Holt Literature & Langua

Introductory Course

TEACHER'S GUIDE
Spelling

- **Instructional Options**
- **Additional Practice**
- **Home Activities**

HOLT, RINEHART AND WINSTON

A Harcourt Classroom Education Company

Austin • New York • Orlando • Atlanta • San Francisco • Boston • Dallas • Toronto • London

STAFF CREDITS

EDITORIAL

Manager of Editorial Operations

Bill Wahlgren

Executive Editor

Emily G. Shenk

Project Editor

James E. Eckel

Writing and Editing

Karen S. Ellis, Michael Nassoiy, Peggy Ferrin, Steve Oelenberger, Jennifer R. Schwan, Stephanie Wenger

Copyediting

Michael Neibergall, *Copyediting Manager;* Mary Malone, *Senior Copyeditor;* Joel Bourgeois, Elizabeth Dickson, Gabrielle Field, Julie A. Hill, Jane Kominek, Millicent Ondras, Theresa Reding, Dennis Scharnberg, Kathleen Scheiner, Laurie Schlesinger, *Copyeditors*

Project Administration

Marie Price, *Managing Editor;* Lori De La Garza, *Editorial Operations Coordinator;* Thomas Browne, Heather Cheyne, Mark Holland, Marcus Johnson, Jill O'Neal, Joyce Rector, Janet Riley, Kelly Tankersley, *Project Administration;* Gail Coupland, Ruth Hooker, Margaret Sanchez, *Word Processing*

Editorial Permissions

Janet Harrington, *Permissions Editor*

ART, DESIGN, AND PHOTO

Graphic Services

Kristen Darby, *Manager*

Image Acquisitions

Joe London, *Director;* Tim Taylor, *Photo Research Supervisor;* Rick Benavides, *Assistant Photo Researcher;* Elaine Tate, *Supervisor;* Erin Cone, *Art Buyer*

Cover Design

Curtis Riker, *Director*
Sunday Patterson, *Designer*

PRODUCTION/ MANUFACTURING

Belinda Barbosa Lopez, *Senior Production Coordinator*
Carol Trammel, *Supervisor*
Beth Prevelige, *Senior Production Manager*

Printed in the United States of America

ISBN 0-03-066129-3

1 2 3 4 5 022 04 03 02 01

Table of Contents

Table of Contents *(continued)*

Table of Contents *(continued)*

Management Charts

Student Worksheets and Answer Key

Teacher Resources

Philosophy of *Spelling*

INTRODUCTION

Spelling presents spelling and vocabulary instruction that is developmental in sequence and comprehensive in scope. Based on extensive research, the program offers teachers useful and practical strategies for maximizing students' learning of spelling and provides numerous opportunities for students to learn and apply a variety of spelling strategies to all of their writing.

BELIEFS

Spelling is based upon these beliefs:

- Use of an organized, developmental spelling curriculum and purposeful activities promotes spelling growth.
- A diagnostic tool that gives teachers insight into each student's stage of development is an integral part of an effective spelling program.
- A spelling program should help students develop a spelling consciousness—an ability to examine their own writing and identify misspelled words.
- Allowing students to invent or use temporary spelling in their writing, while gradually helping them arrive at more standard spellings, reflects the natural developmental process for learning spelling.
- Knowledge of the history and heritage of the English language, along with language play, is an essential component of a spelling program.

CONCEPT LESSONS

Spelling provides instruction and practice for every day of the week. Each core lesson, which can be combined with a Pretest and a Posttest, includes

- a spelling generalization
- a corresponding list of Spelling Words gathered from research
- activities that incorporate one or more graphophonic, visual, or morphemic spelling strategies that students practice and apply to learn to be strategic spellers

REVIEW LESSONS

The last lesson of each unit in *Spelling* is a review lesson that connects to language skills. By reviewing spelling and vocabulary in the context of these activities, students reinforce spelling in a natural way.

Planning Instruction

INSTRUCTIONAL PLAN

The instructional plan of the developmental lessons is both consistent and flexible.

- Skill development takes place in the context of reading, writing, listening, and speaking.
- Students progress through the following stages in each lesson: discovery of spelling patterns through sorting, consideration of relevant rules and strategies, application of these rules and strategies, and confirmation of understanding.
- Suggestions for meeting individual needs help ensure that every student benefits from every lesson.
- Each developmental lesson has two parts that may be taught in 3–5 days.
- Opportunities for teacher choice allow instruction to be tailored to fit the various developmental levels of students.

LESSON PREPARATION

The first page of each Teacher's Guide lesson provides tools for making instruction appropriate for students and includes objectives and lesson-planning information as well as second-language support guidance. The Pretest/Posttest and answers to the Pupil's Edition sorting activity also appear on this page.

INTRODUCING AND TEACHING STRATEGIES

The first page of each lesson also offers a Pretest and a Self-Check procedure. Introducing the Lesson offers two options—Open Sort and Modeling. The open-sort activity allows students to use their own sorting criterion. The modeling activity allows teachers to introduce the lesson skill in context. Teaching the Lesson offers a closed-sort activity that walks through the various patterns represented in the list of Spelling Words.

PRACTICE AND REINFORCEMENT STRATEGIES

This page presents useful strategies and structural information about the Spelling Words. Students immediately put this new knowledge to use in the activities.

Students also have the opportunity to demonstrate proficiency by taking a Posttest. Answers to Spelling Clues, Proofreading, Fun with Words, and Working with Meaning are also included. Reteaching the Lesson provides help for students with learning differences.

UNIT REVIEW LESSONS

The Unit Review Lesson gives students opportunities to work with the words, review strategies and rules, and apply accumulated knowledge.

Meeting Individual Needs

Each lesson in the Teacher's Guide provides research-based support and teaching strategies to help meet the individual needs of students.

LEARNING DIFFERENCES

Many features of *Spelling* encourage application of different learning modalities:

- Reteaching the Lesson is designated for visual, auditory, or kinesthetic learners.
- The Self-Check activities and the open- and closed-sort activities in each lesson also address varying modalities.

SECOND-LANGUAGE SUPPORT

Each Teacher's Guide lesson includes Second-Language Support notes. These notes

- identify patterns and spelling skills that are transferable from certain languages to English
- describe phonemic elements that differ between some students' first language and English
- suggest ways to reinforce and convey the meaning of unfamiliar words and phrases
- encourage students acquiring English to work with peer tutors who can model correct usage and answer questions

The many oral language activities in *Spelling* are also of great benefit to students who are acquiring English.

DEVELOPMENTAL LEVELS

Spelling recognizes that today's classroom includes students at different developmental levels. The Spelling Placement Inventory and the Pretests/Posttests provide insight into each student's developmental level, and each lesson includes suggestions for adapting instruction. See also page ix for help in determining your students' developmental levels.

Developmental Levels of Spellers

Students benefit most from instruction that is appropriate to their developmental levels. The developmental levels of most students may be determined by using the Spelling Placement Inventory on pages xii–xiv of this Teacher's Guide.

TRANSITIONAL SPELLERS
(Below Level)

- These students move from concrete to more abstract representation, one that requires greater reliance on visual memory—spelling words the way they look rather than the way they sound.
- Transitional spellers may include all the appropriate letters in a word, but they may reverse some letters, such as in *TAOD* for *toad* or *FETE* for *feet*.
- Students may still invent spellings, but they have learned many of the conventions of English spelling. They put vowels in every syllable, use vowel digraph patterns, spell inflectional endings correctly, and use English letter sequences that occur frequently.
- By reading, writing, and thinking about spelling, these students develop a sense of when a particular spelling looks correct.

SYNTACTIC-SEMANTIC SPELLERS
(On Level)

- These students are competent and correct spellers. They understand the English spelling system and its basic rules.
- Students understand the accurate spelling of prefixes, suffixes, contractions, compound words, and many irregular spellings; they usually use silent letters and double consonants correctly; they are able to distinguish homophones.
- Through understanding the principles of syllable juncture and applying what they know about one-syllable words, students are able to spell multisyllabic words accurately.
- When spelling a new word, students think of alternative spellings and visualize the word.
- Students begin to recognize word origins and use this information to make meaningful associations as they accumulate a large body of known spellings.

STRATEGIC SPELLERS
(Above Level)

- These students have already mastered basic spelling patterns and are able to apply them automatically.
- Students have developed a spelling consciousness that allows them to adapt and integrate spelling strategies as a natural part of the writing process.
- Their understanding of meaning relationships enables students to be confident language users and serves as a powerful spelling resource.

Assessment

INFORMAL ASSESSMENT OPTIONS

Error Analysis Chart for Writing Activities

The chart on page 86 of this Teacher's Guide enables you to record and analyze the words students misspell as they complete writing activities in each unit. It is designed to help you analyze the nature of students' spelling errors and thereby customize instruction to meet individual needs.

Portfolio Conference

Periodic conferences give students, teachers, and family members a chance to reflect on each student's writing and developing knowledge of spelling. An evaluation portfolio should be created for each student. See Guidelines for Portfolio Conferences on pages xv–xvii for suggestions of items to include in each evaluation portfolio.

Spelling Placement Inventory

See pages xii–xiv for administering and interpreting the Spelling Placement Inventory. The Spelling Placement Inventory will help you devise an instructional plan for each student by assessing his or her developmental level.

FORMAL ASSESSMENT OPTIONS

Pretest/Posttest/Practice Test

The Pretest/Posttest for each lesson provides a set of numbered context sentences for the Spelling Words. Students are asked to write each Spelling Word after hearing the word and its context sentence read aloud.

The Pretest given at the beginning of each lesson encourages students to draw on their prior knowledge. It determines which spelling patterns or generalizations have been mastered and which areas need improvement. The Self-Check activities encourage students to play an active role in evaluating their work. Assign or have students choose partners for assessing students' own words.

The Posttest given at the end of each lesson is an effective diagnostic tool for determining if extra practice is needed. In addition, the Practice Test at the end of each unit may be used to assess student progress.

Assessment *(continued)*

RESEARCH FINDINGS

Research has shown that spelling instruction is most effective when it is linked to authentic writing tasks. For students to develop the skills and habits of proficient spellers, they need to view correct spelling within the broader context of reading, writing, and the communication of ideas. Therefore, the natural starting point for the assessment of spelling awareness is the written work that students complete in all subject areas as part of their daily assignments.

ERROR ANALYSIS CHART

Spelling supports you in the ongoing informal assessment of each student's developing spelling skills. The Error Analysis Chart on page 86 provides space for recording the misspellings that appear in students' writing. Use the chart to help you identify recurring spelling errors, analyze the nature of the misspellings, and determine which lessons in *Spelling* will be of greatest benefit.

As students work through each lesson, mastering spelling and acquiring skills, update the charts. This process will enable you to identify areas of achievement and informally assess areas that need improvement.

INTEGRATED ACTIVITIES

The lessons in *Spelling* are designed to engage students actively in integrated listening, speaking, reading, and writing activities and to help them develop a spelling consciousness. All of the activities provide excellent opportunities for ongoing performance-based assessment. Clues to students' developing word knowledge and attitudes toward spelling may also be revealed in oral summarizing activities. Throughout the lesson, students are encouraged to assess their progress and to help their classmates evaluate their work.

PORTFOLIO ASSESSMENT

To develop independent spelling awareness, *Spelling* teaches spelling as part of the writing process. Writing samples, including unfinished work and proofread drafts, should be included in an evaluation portfolio and reviewed periodically. The proofreading phase provides important clues to students' progress. For informal assessment during this stage, students can work independently, in pairs, or in small groups.

You may want to monitor students' performances, observing how effectively they edit their work and how successfully they select resources to confirm spellings. Students' Personal Word Logs are another useful measure of their growth as independent, competent spellers.

Spelling Placement Inventory

Administering the Spelling Placement Inventory

Administer the Spelling Placement Inventory on page xiv at the beginning of the school year.

1. Dictate the 25 words to students by pronouncing each word, using it in a sentence, and then pronouncing the word again.
2. Collect students' papers and score each Spelling Placement Inventory by writing the correct spelling beside each incorrect spelling. An example follows.

STUDENT 1		STUDENT 2	
interupt	*interrupt*	*inneruped*	*interrupt*
signifigant	*significant*	*cegnfeacint*	*significant*
inscription	✓	*enscrepsion*	*inscription*
neuclei	*nuclei*	*newcleie*	*nuclei*
invisible	✓	*invizabol*	*invisible*
ocuppied	*occupied*	*ocupide*	*occupied*
oval	✓	*oval*	✓
impacient	*impatient*	*impashent*	*impatient*
vital	✓	*vital*	✓
ilegal	*illegal*	*ilegle*	*illegal*

3. Assign a numerical score to each student's Spelling Placement Inventory (0 percent to 100 percent range, with 4 points taken off for each incorrect spelling). At the beginning of the school year, a student should be able to spell at least 30 percent of the list words correctly if he or she is to benefit fully from working in this grade level of *Spelling.*

   Students who spell 30 percent or more of the pretest words correctly will likely produce misspellings that show adequate knowledge of sixth-grade spelling patterns. Student 1, in this example, spelled four of the ten words correctly (40 percent of this sample). Note, however, that each of the misspellings was off by only one feature (e.g., *interupt* for *interrupt, signifigant* for *significant, neuclei* for *nuclei, ocuppied* for *occupied, impacient* for *impatient,* and *ilegal* for *illegal*). Student 1 should benefit from sixth-grade spelling instruction.

Spelling Placement Inventory *(continued)*

Student 2 spelled only two of the ten words correctly (20 percent of this sample). Note further that this student's misspellings, although interpretable, were often considerably off the mark (e.g., *inneruped* for *interrupt*, *impashent* for *impatient*, and *ilegle* for *illegal*). Student 2 lacks spelling-pattern knowledge at the sixth-grade level and could benefit from studying spelling words at a lower grade or difficulty level.

4. By administering the same 25-word Spelling Placement Inventory at the end of this grade level and scoring it in the manner described, you will be able to document for each student pretest/posttest gains in the number of correct spellings and also corresponding pretest-to-posttest change in the quality of the student's misspellings. The Spelling Placement Inventory may also be administered periodically to determine growth over shorter periods.

By the end of the year, an achieving student should score at least 70 percent accuracy on the Spelling Placement Inventory, and the student's errors on the Spelling Placement Inventory should reflect grade-level spelling-pattern knowledge.

Grade 6 Spelling Placement Inventory

Follow the directions on pages xii–xiii for administering this Spelling Placement Inventory.

WORDS	STAGES Errors indicating instructional-level knowledge of the spelling system	Errors indicating below-grade-level knowledge of the spelling system
1. interrupt	interupt	inneruped
2. significant	signifagant	cegnfeacint
3. inscription	inscrippsion	enscrepsion
4. nuclei	neuclei	newcleie
5. invisible	invisable, inviseable	invizabil
6. occupied	occuppied, ocuppied	ocupide, ockewpied
7. oval	ovil, ovel	ovell, oavel
8. impatient	impacient	impashent
9. vital	vitle, vidle	vietele
10. illegal	ilegal	ilecle
11. reins	reines, rains	ranes
12. reproduction	repreduction	repreducshon
13. criminal	crimminal, criminel	cremenle
14. incredible	incredable	inceredebul
15. foreign	foregn	forren
16. token	tokan	toaken
17. committed	comitted, commited	cometed
18. appreciate	apreciate, appresiate	epreeseate
19. commotion	comotion	comotoin
20. preferred	prefered	perferd
21. obedience	obedianse, obbediants	obedens
22. constitution	constatution	constitushun
23. responsibility	responsebility	responsebilaty
24. pleasant	plesant, plessant	plessent
25. opponent	opponant	oponent

Note: At Grades 6–8, the instructional level is the syntactic-semantic level. Below-level students spell at the transitional level. If students achieve higher than 70 percent accuracy on the Spelling Placement Inventory, they may be able to work at the strategic level of instruction.

Guidelines for Portfolio Conferences

Since spelling occurs naturally within the context of writing, a portfolio provides an effective way of illustrating students' development as spellers. This section provides suggestions for including indicators of spelling progress in students' portfolios. It also offers guidelines for discussing spelling progress in conferences with students and with family members.

INCORPORATING SPELLING SAMPLES INTO THE PORTFOLIO

Each student should organize the contents of the portfolio according to a system with which he or she feels comfortable. After students have decided on a method, suggest that they think about ways to include examples of their spelling work. Ask them to decide how their spelling work best fits in with other categories in the portfolio.

If a student has organized a portfolio by topic, he or she may want to place topic-related Spelling Words in the appropriate sections of the portfolio. If a student's portfolio is organized chronologically, spelling-related work might be placed in the portfolio according to when the work was done. Some students may prefer to create a separate section just for spelling work.

ITEMS TO INCLUDE IN A PORTFOLIO

In addition to selecting several examples of completed spelling assignments, students might choose to include the following items in their portfolios:

Writing Samples Encourage students to add writing samples that show spelling corrections they have made. Drafts showing errors that students have discovered and corrected while proofreading are good indicators of their spelling progress.

Pretest and Posttest You may want to have students include Pretests and Posttests in their portfolios to show the progress they have made with particular groups of words. Such items should not be included as part of a formal assessment or as a means of judging students' weaknesses. Rather, the tests should be used as a method of demonstrating progress and as a way for students to assess their own achievements.

Personal Word Logs If students are keeping Personal Word Logs of unusual and interesting words, encourage them to photocopy some of these pages and add them to the portfolio. These pages provide insight into a student's interests.

Learning about a word's origin by studying its root, such as the Latin root *aqua,* may help a student understand and spell a variety of unfamiliar words that share this root, such as *aqua-*

Guidelines for Portfolio Conferences *(continued)*

marine, aquatic, and *aquarium.* Encourage students to record the root in their Personal Word Logs and add the sheet to their portfolios.

CONFERENCES BETWEEN A FAMILY MEMBER AND A TEACHER

Discuss with the family member how the student has chosen to incorporate indicators of his or her spelling progress into the portfolio. Then share examples of the student's work that reveal spelling development, such as writing activities, Personal Word Log pages, and Pretest/Posttest pages. The following checklist may be used to help you emphasize the progress individual students have made and point out areas that need improvement:

- awareness of spelling patterns
- ability to apply knowledge of known words to unfamiliar words that share a similar pattern or origin
- developmental level of the student

CONFERENCES BETWEEN A TEACHER AND A STUDENT

Try to conduct the conferences so that the student does most of the talking. Prompts such as these will help generate discussion:

- Tell me how you organized your spelling work in your portfolio.
- Let's look at a piece of writing that shows some corrections you made in spelling. How did you find the mistakes? How did you figure out how to spell the words correctly?
- What spelling strategies are most helpful to you when you are trying to spell new words?
- How often do you use a dictionary? How is a dictionary helpful?
- What kind of progress do you think you have made in spelling?

The student's responses to questions such as these will provide valuable insight into his or her attitudes, habits, and strengths. Help the student set goals that will develop increased proficiency in spelling. These goals might include using a dictionary more often when proofreading, consulting with peers when troublesome words are encountered, or referring to spelling strategies more often.

CONFERENCES BETWEEN TWO STUDENTS

Peer portfolio conferences offer a valuable opportunity for students to discuss their progress, share the things they find most challenging, and compare problem-solving strategies with one another. The questions on page xvii can help students get their peer conferences off the ground. You might want to duplicate a set of questions for each pair of students to use as a guide during the conference.

Guidelines for Portfolio Conferences *(continued)*

- How did you organize your portfolio?
- Where did you put your spelling work? What kinds of things did you include?
- What do you like about spelling? What is hard about spelling for you?
- What do you do when you want to write a word but don't know how to spell it?
- What are some difficult words you can spell? How did you learn to spell them?

Encourage students to share the strategies they have discovered that are the most useful for spelling new words and remembering the spelling of troublesome words. Ask students to try to be as specific as they can. For example, a student who has trouble with *ie/ei* spellings may have developed a mnemonic device for remembering which spelling to use.

Also, encourage students to become resources for one another in sharing their solutions and strategies. Encourage them to take notes during their peer conferences and add them to the portfolio. Each student's name, his or her partner's name, the date of the conference, and any valuable information learned during the conference should be included.

How to Study a Word

The strategy described in How to Study a Word on Pupil's Edition page v will help students become successful, independent spellers. The strategy utilizes visual, auditory, and kinesthetic modalities.

- The first step has students say the word aloud and think about its meaning, reinforcing the meaning basis for spelling.
- The second step asks students to look at the word, think about words that are related in meaning or resemble the word, and visualize the word. (This step develops the use of analogy as a spelling cue.)
- The third step has students spell the word silently and think about sound-letter relationships, reinforcing sound-letter relationships and sound-letter cues.
- The fourth step utilizes a kinesthetic mode—writing—to develop students' visual memory of the word. Students write the word, check the clarity of the letters, and then rewrite the word if necessary. (This step reminds students to write legibly to avoid spelling errors.)
- The fifth step strengthens students' visual memory of the word by having them cover the word they wrote and check its spelling.

INTRODUCING THE STUDY STEPS

Before students begin their work in the Pupil's Edition, introduce them to How to Study a Word. Have students read page v silently. Ask volunteers to re-read the five steps aloud. Guide students through the steps, using an example.

WAYS TO USE THE STEPS

Discuss with students how they might use How to Study a Word. Here are some suggestions:

- when they encounter unfamiliar words or words they are unsure of how to spell
- when they misspell words in their writing
- when they misspell words on the Pretest or Posttest

Spelling and Proofreading Strategies

The lessons in *Spelling* are designed around and utilize two major strategies of instruction: (a) phonology—consistent spelling patterns based on sound-letter relationships and (b) analogy—common characteristics of words as the basis for predicting the spelling of unfamiliar words.

To aid students in developing the tools to become competent, independent spellers, spelling and proofreading strategies are provided to maximize their learning. The strategies help students think about spelling as a skill they can develop through a variety of processes such as these:

- Utilizing a five-step strategy can help them learn the spelling of new words.
- Using a variety of spelling strategies can help them remember the spelling of troublesome words.
- Using possible spellings, thinking about word families, and using a dictionary can help them figure out how to spell new words.
- Proofreading will help them identify spelling errors in their own writing.

SPELLING STRATEGIES

These specific strategies and others are presented in *Spelling:*

- *How to Study a Word* Students are encouraged to use the five study steps to help them learn the spelling of new words.
- *Picture/Sound Out a Word* In this strategy, students picture a word they want to write and think about the sound a letter stands for.
- *Try Different Spellings* Students think about the vowel sound in a word, consider different ways this sound can be represented by letters, and try different spellings until the word looks right.
- *Guess and Check* Students guess the spelling of a word and then check its spelling in a dictionary.
- *Rhyming Words/Word Families* By thinking about word families or rhyming words that share the same spelling pattern and sound-letter relationship, students often figure out the spelling of a word.
- *Use a Dictionary* Students can simply look up the spelling of a word in a dictionary.
- *Homophones* Students pay particular attention to context clues and make sure homophones are spelled correctly.
- *Compound Words* Students break compound words into two smaller words and check the spelling of each word.
- *Mnemonic Devices/Memory Clues* Good spellers develop and use memory clues, including mnemonic devices, to help them remember the spelling of words.

Spelling and Proofreading Strategies *(continued)*

PROOFREADING STRATEGIES

These particular strategies are helpful to students as they proofread:

- *Proofread Twice* By proofreading their writing twice, students identify spelling errors they know they have made as well as possible misspellings.
- *Proofread with a Partner* Using this strategy, students work with a partner to check and discuss each other's spelling.
- *Proofread Backward* By beginning with the last word in a paragraph and reading each word in isolation, students are apt to notice misspellings because the words are not in context.

INTRODUCING THE STRATEGIES

Ask students to name some strategies they can use to help them figure out how to spell a word that is new to them and to remember the spelling of words they know. List their suggestions on the board. Explain that students will learn about some additional spelling strategies they can use as they write and proofread. Have students read pages vi and vii silently. Then, invite volunteers to read aloud the strategies.

Encourage students to summarize the strategies by asking questions such as these:

- Which strategies might you use when you are trying to figure out how to spell a word you don't know?
- Imagine that you want to spell the word *light*. How can thinking about the words *might* and *bright* help you?
- Imagine that you need to spell the compound word *firehouse*. What strategy could you use to help you?
- How can proofreading your written work two times help you find spelling errors?

Invite students to share mnemonic devices they have heard or made up themselves that help them remember the spelling of new words.

Discuss with students when to use spelling and proofreading strategies. Point out that these strategies are also useful as students are writing. Encourage students to refer to pages vi and vii as they write.

Word Logs

A Word Log provides an excellent opportunity for students to record new words they learn, keep an ongoing record of words they have misspelled on pretests or in other writing, and note troublesome words as an aid to writing and proofreading. A Word Log also encourages students to record words that are of special interest to them, such as words having to do with a favorite activity, place, or topic. The Pupil's Edition of *Spelling* includes Word Logs in which students may record words from the spelling lessons, words they have misspelled in pretests and posttests, and words they acquire from other sources.

INTRODUCING THE WORD LOGS

Ask students to name some different ways they learn new words *(reading books, signs, menus; listening to the radio; watching TV; talking with friends).* To introduce the idea of a Word Log, ask students to name some ways they can remember new words they learn. Explain that there is a special section of their spelling book that they can use for recording new words. Have students read page viii of the Pupil's Edition silently.

Invite students to examine the Word Logs in their books.

CREATING WORD LOGS

You might also have students create additional or separate individual Word Logs. Encourage students to use sheets of lined paper that they can keep in a notebook. To be useful, each Word Log should be organized so that students can easily find words they have written and systematically add new words. Students might organize their logs alphabetically, with one page for each letter of the alphabet.

Encourage students to include these items in their logs:

- troublesome words such as *there, their,* and *they're,* along with context sentences or definitions that help students remember which word to use
- words that share a spelling pattern or common structure
- interesting word facts about word origins and history

Set aside some time for students to create or decorate the covers for their Word Logs.

Lesson 1: Short Vowels

OBJECTIVE

To spell words that demonstrate these sound-letter relationships: /a/a; /e/e; /i/i; /o/o; /u/u

HOME ACTIVITY

The home activity is on page 90.

SECOND-LANGUAGE SUPPORT

Short vowel sounds are often difficult for students with limited English proficiency. For example, students have trouble differentiating the vowel sounds heard in words such as *bat* and *bet*. The vowel sound in *cot* causes difficulty for students who speak Spanish, Chinese, Vietnamese, Tagalog, and Thai. Write word pairs such as *bat/bet, sat/set, man/men, cot/cut,* and *shot/shut* on the board. Have students pronounce each pair of words, stressing the vowel sound in each word. COMPARING AND CONTRASTING

PRETEST/POSTTEST

1. Put all the food into the **sack.**
2. I **admit** that I'm afraid of spiders.
3. The train traveled at a **rapid** speed.
4. I will **glance** at the article about this book later.
5. I will **contact** you later this week.
6. Dave signed a one-year **contract** with the company.
7. The soldiers **advance** toward the fort.
8. You can measure the **depth** of the pond with a ruler.
9. I will make a **comment** on the game after it is over.
10. We climbed to the **summit** of the mountain.
11. The inventor will **sketch** her machine on paper.
12. His ideas sound like a great deal of **nonsense** to me.

(continued on next page)

Pretest

Administer the test on this page as a pretest. Say each word, use it in the sentence, and then repeat the word. ACCESSING PRIOR KNOWLEDGE

SELF-CHECK Have students check their own pretests against the list of Spelling Words. Remind students to write misspelled words in their Lesson Word Logs. STUDENT SELF-ASSESSMENT

Introducing the Lesson

Option A (Open Sort)

Distribute the word cards (page 89) to individuals or small groups, and guide them in an open-sort activity. In open sort, students group the word cards according to a criterion they select themselves. They might group words that share the same beginning or middle sound, words that are related by topic, or words that have a similar shape.

Option B (Modeling)

Read aloud with students the lesson title and the Spelling Words. Use this model sentence to introduce the lesson skill in a context.

*Open the **flap** on the **tent**.*

Teaching the Lesson

- Ask volunteers to name one-syllable Spelling Words that have the same vowel sound as they hear in *bat*. *(sack, glance)* Then, have students name two-syllable Spelling Words with the same sound. *(rapid, contact, contract, advance, admit)*
- Follow the same procedure with words having the short *e, i, o,* and *u* sounds. *(/e/: depth, sketch, comment, ethnic, nonsense, splendid; /i/: rapid, admit, ethnic, splendid, summit, liquid, impulse; /o/: contact, contract, comment, nonsense; /u/: summit, impulse)*

IN SUMMARY You may want students to summarize the lesson in their own words. Elicit from students that a short vowel sound is often spelled with only one vowel letter. Students can use this sound-letter pattern to predict how to write a word when they don't know how to spell it.

ASSIGNMENT Students can complete the first page of the lesson as a follow-up to the group activity, either in class or as homework.

Lesson 1: Short Vowels *(continued)*

Practicing the Lesson

Spelling Clues: Listening to Short Vowels

Suggest that when students say a word aloud, they stress the vowel sound and listen carefully for the exact sound being made. Remind students that in many cases, the short vowel sound is spelled with a single letter that matches the sound—that is, *a* for short *a*; *e* for short *e*; and so on.

Remind students that another way to figure out the spelling of a short vowel sound is to think of other words that rhyme with the word in question. For example, if students know that the short *a* sound in the word *act* is spelled with the letter *a*, they can then figure out that *contact* and *contract* are also spelled with the letter *a*. APPLYING SPELLING STRATEGIES

Proofreading

You may wish to have students review Spelling Clues: Listening to Short Vowels before proofreading the road signs.

Fun with Words

Students may complete this activity independently or with a partner. Tell students to use Spelling Words they have not already used on lines 1–12. They can use the Spelling Dictionary to check word meanings.

SECOND-LANGUAGE SUPPORT Pair students, and have each partner read the dialogue of one of the cartoon characters. Then have students explain the meaning and the humor of the cartoon. USING CONTEXT CLUES

Posttest

Administer the test on page xxii as a posttest, or administer one of your own. Say each word, use it in a sentence, and then repeat the word.

Reteaching the Lesson

Have students write each Spelling Word on a separate index card. Pair students and tell them to shuffle all their cards together and then sort the words according to their vowel sounds (long *a*, long *e*, long *i*, and long *o*). Have one student hold up a card; have the other student look at the word, say and spell it aloud, and then say the letters that spell the long-vowel sounds. The second student should then close his or her eyes, say the word again, and respell the entire word. The partner should then confirm whether or not the spelling is correct. KINESTHETIC MODALITY

(Pretest/Posttest, continued)

13. You did a **splendid** job on your speech today.
14. We studied the **ethnic** backgrounds of different peoples.
15. Ice turns to **liquid** when it melts.
16. On an **impulse,** I decided to call an old friend.

PRACTICE ACTIVITY

The practice activity is on page 91.

Answers: Spelling Clues

1. contract
2. comment
3. liquid
4. nonsense
5. sack
6. ethnic

Answers: Proofreading

7. summit
8. splendid
9. rapid
10. contact
11. advance
12. depth

Answers: Fun with Words

13. admit
14. glance
15. sketch
16. impulse

Lesson 2: Long Vowels

OBJECTIVE

To spell words that have a long vowel sound

HOME ACTIVITY

The home activity is on page 93.

SECOND-LANGUAGE SUPPORT

Students whose first language is Spanish, Chinese, Vietnamese, Tagalog, or Thai frequently have difficulty with long vowel words, because they find it hard to differentiate such words from short-vowel words. For example, they might pronounce *coat* and *cot* the same way. Also, the letters *oa* in Spanish words represent two different sounds, so Spanish-speaking students may not pronounce English *oa* as long *o*. Have students brainstorm English words having long vowel sounds. Write each word on the board, and have students underline the letters that spell the long vowel sound. COMPARING AND CONTRASTING

PRETEST/POSTTEST

1. Worms are a popular **bait** for catching fish.
2. The **peach** was ripe and juicy.
3. The **bride** was smiling at the groom in the picture.
4. Potatoes are a **prime** crop for the state of Idaho.
5. The explorer has been to almost every country on the **globe.**
6. Look at the rows of trees in the orange **grove.**
7. The **slope** is very steep and dangerous to climb.
8. I will **slice** the cake in half.
9. Dad will **roast** a turkey for the main course.
10. The railroad workers drove each **spike** into the ground.

(continued on next page)

Pretest

Administer the test on this page as a pretest. Say each word, use it in the sentence, and then repeat the word. ACCESSING PRIOR KNOWLEDGE

SELF-CHECK Have students check their own pretests against the list of Spelling Words. Remind students to write misspelled words in their Lesson Word Logs. STUDENT SELF-ASSESSMENT

Introducing the Lesson

Option A (Open Sort)

Distribute the word cards (page 92) to individuals or small groups, and guide them in an open-sort activity. In open sort, students group the word cards according to a criterion they select themselves. Then, guide students in comparing and discussing the criteria they selected.

Option B (Modeling)

Read aloud with students the lesson title and the Spelling Words. Use this model sentence to introduce the lesson skill in a context.

*A **lake** is smaller than a **sea**.*

Teaching the Lesson

- Ask students to name Spelling Words that have the same vowel sound as they hear in *kite.* As students name words, list them on the board under *kite. (bride, prime, slice, spike, thigh)* Follow the same procedure with the words *sea, lake,* and *boat. (**sea:** peach, squeeze, breathe; **lake:** bait, praise; **boat:** globe, grove, slope, stroke, roast, gross)*
- After students have named words, have them sort the words under each heading according to the different spelling patterns for that vowel sound.
- After students have added words to the columns from their own writing, have volunteers read aloud all the words and underline the spelling of each long vowel sound.

IN SUMMARY You may want students to summarize the lesson in their own words. Elicit from students that a long vowel sound is usually spelled with two or more letters in combination. Students can use these sound-letter patterns to predict how to write a word when they are not sure of its spelling.

ASSIGNMENT Students can complete the first page of the lesson as a follow-up to the group activity, either in class or as homework.

Lesson 2: Long Vowels *(continued)*

Practicing the Lesson

Spelling Clues: Long Vowel Sounds

Suggest that when students spell a word having a long vowel sound, they check that they have written the vowel itself. Then, if the word looks as if it is spelled wrong, they should add other letters that may, in combination, spell the vowel sound. Caution students about using the strategy of rhyming words in order to guess the correct spelling of a word having a long-vowel sound. This strategy works better with short-vowel words, because in many cases short-vowel sounds have only one spelling. Long-vowel sounds have many more possibilities, however. For example, long *o* might be spelled *o* (*gross*), *oa* (*soap*), *o_e* (*hope*), or *ow* (*tow*). Suggest that students check a dictionary when they're unsure of the spelling of a word with a long-vowel sound. APPLYING SPELLING STRATEGIES

Proofreading

You may wish to have students review Spelling Clues: Long Vowel Sounds before proofreading the sentences.

Fun with Words

Remind students that the second word in each word pair is a Spelling Word. If they cannot figure out the first word, they might want to use the second word as a hint for the first word.

TRANSITIONAL SPELLERS Have students complete this activity with a partner. Students might have difficulty spelling *breath* because the short *e* sound is spelled with a combination of letters. Suggest that they first spell *breathe* and then spell *breath*.

Posttest

Administer the test on page 2 as a posttest, or administer one of your own. Say each word, use it in a sentence, and then repeat the word.

Reteaching the Lesson

Divide the Spelling Words into lists, one for each different long vowel sound heard in the words. First, say each word, emphasizing the long vowel sound. Then, dictate the spelling while students write the word. Next, simultaneously spell the word with students as they write it again. Have students trace the word for additional reinforcement. Finally, have students spell the word aloud as they write it from recall. KINESTHETIC/AUDITORY MODALITIES

(Pretest/Posttest, continued)

11. You can move quickly in the water if you **stroke** your arms fast.
12. The teacher gave much **praise** to the students who tried hardest.
13. If you **squeeze** the tube, the paste will come out.
14. People **breathe** all day without thinking about it.
15. A **gross** equals twelve dozen.
16. The runner had to quit the race after hurting his **thigh.**

PRACTICE ACTIVITY

The practice activity is on page 94.

Answers: Spelling Clues

1. gross
2. thigh
3. spike
4. bride
5. roast
6. grove

Answers: Proofreading

7. peach
8. squeeze
9. slope
10. stroke
11. slice
12. praise

Answers: Fun with Words

13. bat/bait
14. prim/prime
15. breath/breathe
16. glob/globe

TEACHING STRATEGIES

Lesson 3: Variant Vowels

OBJECTIVE

To spell words that demonstrate these sound-letter relationships: */ou/ou; /ô/o, a, au, aw; /o͞o/ou, oo, u*

HOME ACTIVITY

The home activity is on page 96.

SECOND-LANGUAGE SUPPORT

The vowel sound /ô/, as in *salt*, can cause difficulty for students of limited English proficiency whose first language is Spanish, Chinese, Vietnamese, Tagalog, or Thai. Many students have a hard time hearing the difference between /ô/ and /o/. Encourage students to brainstorm words having the /ô/ sound, and then have them brainstorm words having the /o/ sound. Write the words on the board, and let volunteers say each word aloud, stressing the vowel sound and underlining the letters that spell the sound. COMPARING AND CONTRASTING

PRETEST/POSTTEST

1. The children learned to **count** to 100.
2. Many cities and towns may be in the same **county.**
3. Add **salt** to the soup to give it more flavor.
4. Drivers use the bridge to **cross** the river.
5. You'll have to **shout** so I can hear you in the crowd.
6. The school has a special club for any **youth** interested in chess.
7. The final **amount** was over one hundred dollars.
8. How many **pounds** does a baby elephant weigh?
9. Be careful when you climb up the **mountain.**
10. There were **thousands** of fans at the baseball game.

(continued on next page)

Pretest

Administer the test on this page as a pretest. Say each word, use it in the sentence, and then repeat the word. ACCESSING PRIOR KNOWLEDGE

SELF-CHECK Have students check their own pretests against the list of Spelling Words. Remind students to write misspelled words in their Lesson Word Logs. STUDENT SELF-ASSESSMENT

Introducing the Lesson

Option A (Open Sort)

Distribute the word cards (page 95) to individuals or small groups, and guide them in an open-sort activity. In open sort, students group the word cards according to a criterion they select themselves. Then, guide students in comparing and discussing the criteria they selected.

Option B (Modeling)

Read aloud with students the lesson title and the Spelling Words. Use this model sentence to introduce the lesson skill in a context.

*The child **lost** a **tooth.***

Teaching the Lesson

- Ask volunteers to name some words that have the same vowel sound as they hear in *south*. As students name words, list them on the board. After students have named words, have them identify those words in which the /ou/ sound is spelled *ou*. *(count, county, shout, amount, pounds, mountain, thousands, account)*
- Follow the same procedure with /ô/ words spelled *o*, *a*, *au*, or *aw* *(cross, salt, launched, saucer, crawled)*. Have students identify the words having each different spelling pattern. Then repeat the procedure with /o͞o/ words spelled *oo*, *ou*, or *u*. *(proof, youth, rumors)*

IN SUMMARY You may want students to summarize the lesson in their own words. Elicit from students that /ou/, /ô/, and /o͞o/ can be spelled in several different ways; students can use these sound-letter patterns to predict how to write a word when they are not sure of its spelling.

ASSIGNMENT Students can complete the first page of the lesson as a follow-up to the group activity, either in class or as homework.

Lesson 3: Variant Vowels *(continued)*

Practicing the Lesson

Spelling Clues: Reading Aloud

Suggest that when students study a word, they concentrate on shapes of the letters. They should close their eyes and try to see the shapes in their minds. Visualizing the shapes will help them spell the word on paper.

Point out that the /ou/ sound is usually spelled *ou* when the sound comes at the beginning or in the middle of the word (for example, *ounce, found*). Words having /ou/ at the end of the word usually have the sound spelled *ow* (as in *cow*). With the /ô/ and /o͞o/ sounds, several spelling possibilities exist. After students study a word they've written to see whether it looks right, they should check a dictionary if they're still not sure of the spelling. APPLYING SPELLING STRATEGIES

TRANSITIONAL SPELLERS Have students complete this activity with a partner. Each student can check his or her partner's spelling of each word.

Proofreading

You may wish to have students review Spelling Clues: Reading Aloud before proofreading the paragraph.

Fun with Words

Tell students to use Spelling Words they have not already used on lines 1–12. They can use the Spelling Dictionary if they are unsure of the meaning of a word.

SECOND-LANGUAGE SUPPORT Have students read the cartoon dialogue with a partner. Then have them explain the humor of the conversation. RECOGNIZING HUMOR

Posttest

Administer the test on page 4 as a posttest, or administer one of your own. Say each word, use it in a sentence, and then repeat the word.

Reteaching the Lesson

Have students divide the Spelling Words into lists, one for each different spelling pattern. Invite students, one at a time, to read aloud the words in each column of the chart. Ask them to stress the vowel sound each time they pronounce a word. As they say the word, have them use a finger to underline the letters in the word that spell the vowel sound. Then, have students say the entire word one last time and spell it aloud. AUDITORY/KINESTHETIC MODALITIES

(Pretest/Posttest, continued)

11. The scientist found **proof** to support her theory.
12. The snake **crawled** along the side of the road.
13. The witness gave a detailed **account** of what happened.
14. The rocket should not be **launched** in bad weather.
15. There are **rumors** of a surprise test today.
16. Gently place the cup on the **saucer.**

PRACTICE ACTIVITY

The practice activity is on page 97.

Answers: Spelling Clues

1. youth
2. crawled
3. cross
4. salt
5. pounds
6. amount

Answers: Proofreading

7. shout
8. launched
9. thousands
10. count
11. account
12. mountain

Answers: Fun with Words

13. rumors
14. county
15. proof
16. saucer

Lesson 4: Vowels Before *r*

OBJECTIVE

To spell words that demonstrate these sound-letter relationships: /är/*ar;* /âr/*ar, are;* /ôr/*oar, ar, our;* /ûr/*ur, or, er*

HOME ACTIVITY

The home activity is on page 99.

SECOND-LANGUAGE SUPPORT

Some students with limited English proficiency, including speakers of Japanese, Chinese, Korean, Vietnamese, and Thai, may have difficulty differentiating the /r/ sound from the /l/ sound. For example, they may pronounce *purse* as *pulse.* Write each Spelling Word on a separate index card. Hold up the card, and have students pronounce the word aloud, stressing the /r/ sound in each word. Have students underline the letters that make the vowel *-r* sound in each word. IDENTIFYING SOUNDS

PRETEST/POSTTEST

1. The fans **roar** their approval.
2. Keep the dog and cat **apart** during the trip.
3. There is a **reward** for the return of the missing watch.
4. Mary felt **worse** after hearing the bad news.
5. The **turtle** slowly made its way across the road.
6. The young boy had a **nightmare** about a monster.
7. The meat was **burnt.**
8. Wait at the **curb** for the next bus.
9. How much money do you have in your **purse**?
10. In court people often **declare** that they are innocent.
11. Some kinds of fruit are **scarce** in winter.
12. John **inserts** the key into the lock.

(continued on next page)

Pretest

Administer the test on this page as a pretest. Say each word, use it in the sentence, and then repeat the word. ACCESSING PRIOR KNOWLEDGE

SELF-CHECK Have students check their own pretests against the list of Spelling Words. Remind students to write misspelled words in their Lesson Word Logs. STUDENT SELF-ASSESSMENT

Introducing the Lesson

Option A (Open Sort)

Distribute the word cards (page 98) to individuals or small groups, and guide them in an open-sort activity. In open sort, students group the word cards according to a criterion they select themselves. Then, guide students in comparing and discussing the criteria they selected.

Option B (Modeling)

Read aloud with students the lesson title and the Spelling Words. Use this model sentence to introduce the lesson skill in a context.

*Choose **verbs** with **care** when you write.*

Teaching the Lesson

- Ask volunteers to name some words that have the same vowel *-r* sound as they hear in *start.* As students name words, have them identify the letters that spell the /är/ sound. *(apart, sparkling, warrant)*
- Follow the same procedure with /âr/, /ôr/, and /ûr/. After students have named words, have them sort the words with different spellings on the board under the headings *stare (nightmare, declare, scarce); soar (roar, reward, source);* and *lurch (turtle, burnt, curb, purse, worse, inserts, nervous).*
- After students have added to the columns words from their own writing, have volunteers read aloud all the words and underline the spelling of each vowel *-r* sound.

IN SUMMARY You may want students to summarize the lesson in their own words. Elicit from students that the sounds /är/, /âr/, /ôr/, and /ûr/ can be spelled in several ways; students can use these sound-letter patterns to predict how to write a word when they are not sure of its spelling.

ASSIGNMENT Students can complete the first page of the lesson as a follow-up to the group activity, either in class or as homework.

Lesson 4: Vowels Before *r* *(continued)*

Practicing the Lesson

Spelling Clues: Comparing Spellings

Suggest that after students have written a word several different ways, they first eliminate those spellings they are positive are incorrect. Then they can look more closely at the remaining possibilities before making a final choice.

Point out that since the /är/ sound has one basic spelling (*ar*), that is the most likely spelling to try for such words. The /ôr/ and /ûr/ sounds have at least three possible spellings each, however. Students can try each spelling (for example, spelling *roar, rar*, and *rour*, or spelling *worse, wurse*, and *werse*) before making a decision. APPLYING SPELLING STRATEGIES

Proofreading

You may wish to have students review Spelling Clues: Comparing Spellings before proofreading the phone message.

Working with Meaning

Students may complete this activity individually or with a partner. Remind students that the pictures can help them determine which words to choose.

SECOND-LANGUAGE SUPPORT Pair students and have each partner read one character's dialogue from the cartoon. Encourage students to point out context clues that helped them know which words to supply in the sentences. USING CONTEXT CLUES

Posttest

Administer the test on page 6 as a posttest, or administer one of your own. Say each word, use it in a sentence, and then repeat the word.

Reteaching the Lesson

Have students create a chart for reinforcing the unusual ways of spelling the vowel sounds taught in this lesson. Make the boxes big enough to enable them to write in each box five or six words that use the spelling pattern. Read aloud each Spelling Word, one at a time. Call on volunteers to correctly spell the words and place them in the box with the corresponding spelling pattern. When the Spelling Words have been correctly written in the boxes, display the chart. Have volunteers add to appropriate boxes more words that exemplify the spelling patterns as they encounter them in their reading or writing. VISUAL MODALITY

(Pretest/Posttest, continued)

13. The **sparkling** stars look like diamonds in the sky.
14. What is the **source** of your information?
15. I always get **nervous** before a big test.
16. A **warrant** is out for his arrest.

PRACTICE ACTIVITY

The practice activity is on page 100.

Answers: Spelling Clues

1. apart
2. inserts
3. scarce
4. purse
5. declare
6. curb

Answers: Proofreading

7. source
8. burnt
9. worse
10. warrant
11. reward

Answers: Working with Meaning

12. turtle
13. nervous
14. sparkling
15. roar
16. nightmare

Unit 1 Review

OBJECTIVES

- To review spelling patterns and strategies in Lessons 1–4
- To give students the opportunity to recognize and use these spelling patterns and Spelling Words in their writing

UNIT 1 WORDS

The following words are reviewed in Practice Test, Parts A and B.

Lesson 1: Short Vowels

rapid
sketch
liquid
depth
comment
nonsense

Lesson 2: Long Vowels

roast
thigh
bait
slice
squeeze
praise

Lesson 3: Variant Vowels

account
rumors
shout
mountain

Lesson 4: Vowels Before *r*

nervous
declare
roar
turtle

Review Strategies

Review with students the following spelling-clue strategies for Lessons 1–4.

Lesson 1 Spelling Clues: Listening to Short Vowels

Say the word *comment* aloud. Ask students to repeat the word with you. Have volunteers identify the short vowel sounds they hear (short *o*, short *e*) and suggest ways those short vowel sounds might be spelled. Then have a volunteer spell the word correctly on the board. Follow the same procedure with *ethnic*. Remind students that it is helpful to listen for vowel sounds in a word before spelling it.

Lesson 2 Spelling Clues: Long Vowel Sounds

Write *r____st* on the board, and say the word *roast*. Ask students to identify the vowel sound they hear (long *o*) and to suggest possible ways of spelling that sound. Then have volunteers write the correct spelling on the board. Remind students always to check the letter or combination of letters they have used to spell the long vowel sound in a word.

Lesson 3 Spelling Clues: Reading Aloud

Ask students to close their eyes. Say the word *launched*, and tell them to picture the word in their minds. Then have them open their eyes and write down the spelling they pictured in their minds. Invite volunteers to write their responses on the board (for example, *lanched, lonched, launched*). Ask students which spelling looks correct. Remind students that visualizing a word before writing it can help in spelling the word.

Lesson 4 Spelling Clues: Comparing Spellings

Write on the board *I have something to declair.* Ask students to find the misspelled word (*declair*) and to suggest ways to spell it correctly (for example, *diclare* or *declare*). Write responses on the board, and then have students identify the correct spelling. Remind them that when they are unsure of a word's spelling, it is helpful to compare different spellings and choose the one that looks right.

Unit 1 Review *(continued)*

Practice Test

The Practice Test provides an opportunity to review Spelling Words and spelling generalizations in a standardized test format, complete with a sample answer card.

Option 1

Use Practice Test: Part A as a pretest. Later, use Practice Test: Part B as a posttest.

Option 2

Have students review their Lesson Word Log for this unit. If they need extra help, you may wish to review the spelling generalizations discussed in the individual lessons. Then administer both parts of the Practice Test to determine whether students have mastered the spelling generalizations.

Practice Test: Part A

1. (B) rapid
2. (A) sketch
3. (D) liquid
4. (D) turtle
5. (C) depth
6. (B) mountain
7. (A) roast
8. (C) thigh
9. (D) bait
10. (D) slice

Practice Test: Part B

1. (A) acount [account]
2. (D) squeaze [squeeze]
3. (D) roumers [rumors]
4. (B) praize [praise]
5. (C) nervus [nervous]
6. (B) showt [shout]
7. (C) declair [declare]
8. (D) nonsence [nonsense]
9. (A) coment [comment]
10. (A) roor [roar]

Options for Evaluation

- Have students check their own Practice Tests against their lists of Spelling Words. The list on the opposite page provides references to the lessons where they can find words they misspelled.
- You may prefer to assign partners and have students check each other's Practice Tests, using their own list of Spelling Words.

REVIEW ACTIVITIES

Activity 1

Have students choose a word from this review lesson to pantomime for classmates. The pantomimes may hint at the word's meaning, spelling, or both. For example, for the word *liquid*, a student might pretend to be drinking water. The person who guesses the word must also spell it correctly before getting the chance to perform the next pantomime.

Activity 2

For students who need reteaching, create a large chart of vowel sounds for the classroom wall. Then invite each student to choose a word from this review lesson, say it aloud, and indicate where it belongs on the chart, based on its vowel sound or sounds. Words with more than one syllable can be entered more than once.

Activity 3

Let students each create a riddle for a word from this review lesson. Give this example: "This word refers to a part of the body. It rhymes with *high*. What is it?" (*thigh*) Invite volunteers to read their riddles aloud. See which listeners can guess the riddle first. Let one of the students who guessed correctly be the one to share a new riddle with the class.

Activity 4

Organize students into small groups. Have one member of each group say aloud a one-syllable word, such as *roast*, and then give group members time to write down words that rhyme with it. Later, have group members say their words and tell whether the spelling of the vowel sound in each word matches that of the original word (*roast* and *toast*, for example) or if the spelling is different (*roast* and *most*, for example).

Unit 1 Review *(continued)*

WHAT'S IN A WORD?

ET

Have students work in small groups to brainstorm titles of science fiction stories. You may wish to let them include movies and television shows as well as books and short stories. Students can also find more titles in the card catalog of the library.

WORKING TOGETHER You may wish to have students work in small groups to choose one of the science fiction titles to illlustrate. Suggest that they make a three-dimensional model of their title illustration.

grasshopper/cricket

If students do not know many, or any, stories or books with grasshoppers and crickets, they might do research in the school library to learn of other titles.

Unit Activity Options

Imaginative Words

When inventing words, students may find it helpful to first list suffixes that can change words into nouns. For example, the suffixes *-ian, -ator, -ness,* and *-er* could be used to create imaginary nouns such as *splendidian, sketchator, impulseness,* and *depther.*

Partner Spelling

If a student writes the wrong answer for a partner's clue, have the first student explain his or her reasoning. Then let the partner rewrite the clue to make it clearer.

Picture Clues

Ask students to select three Spelling Words for this activity and to work independently to draw their clues. Then have students exchange clues with partners. Invite volunteers to share drawings with other students.

Proofreading Partners

Encourage partners to discuss their ideas for paragraphs. Remind them that, to include the listed words, they may need to create an unusual or even a fantastic situation in their paragraphs.

Spelling Partners

Encourage partners to continue playing until all the flashcards have been collected. If a student misspells a word the first time around, have the partner show him or her the same card later, and let the speller try again.

What *Is* in a Word?

You may want to suggest that students look up the history of other words they have come across in their reading. Allow time for them to share their findings with the class.

Endurance Spelling

You may want to suggest that partners keep a record of words that are misspelled so that these words can be reviewed.

Unit 1 Review *(continued)*

Curriculum Options

Health: First-Aid Posters

Organize students into small groups. Assign each group a particular first-aid technique to research (for example, how to bandage a cut, how to treat a burn, or how to administer mouth-to-mouth resuscitation). Group members should find out the exact step-by-step procedure to follow in that type of emergency. Then have students create posters that inform readers what to do in case of emergencies. Use as many Spelling Words as possible on the posters. Later, hang the posters around the classroom so that others can benefit from the information.

Language Arts: Vowel Search

This game is played with five students. Assign the first student the short *a* sound; the second student the short *e* sound; the third, short *i*; the fourth, short *o*; and the fifth, short *u*. Have all five students turn to the same page in a book, such as a reading book or a social studies textbook. Setting a time limit, such as five minutes, challenge students to find and list as many words on the page as they can that use the sound they have been assigned. When the time limit is up, let players switch sounds and do a second search. Each student gets one point for every word found during the first search, and two points from the second search for every word not found by the previous student. The winner is the student who ends up with the most points.

Social Studies: Trial Reenactment

Organize students into groups of four to eight members each. Have each group research a legal case, either one from history that might be described in their social studies textbook or one from a current newspaper. Challenge students to reenact the court case, with individuals portraying the defendant, the prosecuting attorney, the defense attorney, the judge, and the witnesses involved in the case. Students should prepare a script to follow during their reenactment. Ask them to use as many Spelling Words as possible in their script. After group members have rehearsed, they can present their trial reenactment for classmates.

WHAT'S IN A WORD?

phantom

Students may wish to create with a partner or a small group a list of "phantom" people, places, and things from literature. Encourage students to identify the elements that make each example imaginary.

WORKING TOGETHER Have students work in small groups to brainstorm synonyms for *phantom* and *imaginary*. Students may find it useful to search a thesaurus to locate additional synonyms. Encourage students to create sentences using each word to help show whether the word's connotation is positive or negative.

prejudice

You might have students check a dictionary to see how many different meanings they can find for the word *prejudice*.

WORKING TOGETHER Have students, working in small groups, brainstorm lists of books, stories, and plays in which a character faces prejudice. Later, have each group member describe one example of prejudice, using the words *judge* and *before* in the explanation.

Lesson 6: Other Vowel Spellings

OBJECTIVE

To spell words that include unusual spellings of the short *i*, short *u*, long *a*, and long *o* vowel sounds

HOME ACTIVITY

The home activity is on page 102.

SECOND-LANGUAGE SUPPORT

Speakers of other languages may find it hard to recognize that the same vowel sound can be spelled in several different ways. The problem is further complicated when there are silent letters *(although, sleigh)* or when the vowel sound is spelled with a different vowel *(busy, among)*. Divide the Spelling Words into lists that contain the same sound-letter correspondences. If you like, add other words to the lists. (For example, you might include *cymbal, mystery*, and *rhythm* in a list with *system*.) Have students say the word, trace over each letter while saying its name, say the word again, and write the word while saying it. MAKING SOUND-LETTER CORRESPONDENCES

PRETEST/POSTTEST

1. Sal is **busy** doing homework.
2. She lived **among** the animals.
3. That **building** has fifty stories.
4. Beth is too **young** to go.
5. Have you eaten **enough** food?
6. Even **though** he practiced, he didn't make the team.
7. Draw a **straight** line from the apple to the tree.
8. They traveled through a **rough**, unexplored land.
9. It took **courage** to speak up the way she did.
10. My sister is in the **eighth** grade.
11. He has a **system** for getting his homework done.
12. We won the game by fourteen points **although** we were behind at halftime.

(continued on next page)

Pretest

Administer the test on this page as a pretest. Say each word, use it in the sentence, and then repeat the word. ACCESSING PRIOR KNOWLEDGE

SELF-CHECK Have students check their own pretests against the list of Spelling Words. Remind students to write misspelled words in their Lesson Word Logs. STUDENT SELF-ASSESSMENT

Introducing the Lesson

Option A (Open Sort)

Distribute the word cards (page 101) to individuals or small groups, and guide them in an open-sort activity. In open sort, students group the word cards according to a criterion they select themselves. Then, guide students in comparing and discussing the criteria they selected.

Option B (Modeling)

Read aloud with students the lesson title and the Spelling Words. Use this model sentence to introduce the lesson skill in a context.

Her **business** survived the **tough** times.

Teaching the Lesson

- Ask volunteers to name some Spelling Words that have the same vowel sound as they hear in *gym*. As students name words, list them on the board under *gym*. *(busy, building, system, biscuit, courage)*
- Follow the same procedure with the unusual spellings for the short *u* sound and the long *a* and long *o* sounds. You might want to use *tongue* and *weigh* to head the first two of these columns. Have students choose a Spelling Word as a heading for the long *o* column. *(straight, eighth, sleigh, among, young, enough, rough, though, although, boulder, dough)*
- After students have added words from their own reading or writing, have volunteers read aloud all the words and underline the letters that spell the vowel sounds.

IN SUMMARY Encourage students to summarize the lesson in their own words. Elicit from students that vowel sounds occasionally are spelled with unexpected letter combinations. Knowing these sound-letter correspondences can help students spell unfamiliar words.

ASSIGNMENT Students can complete the first page of the lesson as a follow-up to the group activity, either in class or as homework.

Lesson 6: Other Vowel Spellings *(continued)*

Practicing the Lesson

Spelling Clues: Word Shapes

Point out that in spelling words that have unusual spelling patterns, students should apply any strategy that helps them remember the correct spelling. Strategies include looking for small words in bigger ones (like *eight* in eight*h*) and remembering word shapes (for example, that *system* has one letter that goes below the line and one letter that goes above the line). Have students print their Spelling Words neatly and then draw a box that defines the shape of the word around each word. Tell them to try to remember the shape the word makes. Remind students that the sound-letter patterns in this lesson represent unusual ways of spelling vowel sounds. The short *i* sound is usually spelled with an *i* as in *kid*, *thing*, and *big*. Ask them to name other ways to spell the short *i* sound taught in this lesson (*u*, *ui*, *y*, and *a*). APPLYING SPELLING STRATEGIES

Proofreading

You may wish to have students review Spelling Clues: Word Shapes before proofreading the paragraphs.

Working with Meaning

Students may complete this activity individually or with a partner. You may want to follow up this activity by having students create hidden-object pictures for their classmates and write directions that use Spelling Words. PICTURE CLUES

Posttest

Administer the test on page 12 as a posttest, or administer one of your own. Say each word, use it in a sentence, and then repeat the word.

Reteaching the Lesson

Have students create a chart for reinforcing the unusual ways of spelling the vowel sounds taught in this lesson. Make the boxes big enough to enable them to write in each box five or six words that use the spelling pattern. Read aloud each Spelling Word, one at a time. Call on volunteers to correctly spell the words and place them in the box with the corresponding spelling pattern. When the Spelling Words have been correctly written in the boxes, display the chart. Have volunteers add to appropriate boxes more words that exemplify the spelling patterns as they encounter the words in their reading or writing. VISUAL MODALITY

(Pretest/Posttest, continued)

13. We rode across the snowy fields in a **sleigh.**

14. Look out for the **boulder** rolling down the mountain!

15. Would you like cornbread or a **biscuit** with your stew?

16. We twisted the bread **dough** into interesting shapes.

PRACTICE ACTIVITY

The practice activity is on page 103.

Answers: Spelling Clues

1. young
2. sleigh
3. system
4. though
5. eighth
6. boulder

Answers: Proofreading

7. rough
8. busy
9. dough
10. although
11. biscuit

Answers: Working with Meaning

12. among
13. building
14. enough
15. courage
16. straight

Lesson 7: Words with *ie* and *ei*

OBJECTIVE

To spell words that include the vowel combination *ie* or *ei*

HOME ACTIVITY

The home activity is on page 105.

SECOND-LANGUAGE SUPPORT

Since in many languages sound-letter correspondences are consistent from word to word, letter combinations such as *ie* and *ei* can be confusing. Divide the Spelling Words into lists that have the same sound-letter correspondences. If you like, add other words to the lists. (For example, you might add *sleigh*, *neighbor*, and *reign* to the list that includes *reins*.) Have students say the word, trace over each letter while saying its name, say the word again, and write the word while saying it. MAKING SOUND-LETTER CORRESPONDENCES

PRETEST/POSTTEST

1. My mother married her college **boyfriend.**
2. My best **girlfriend** moved away.
3. My cousins get into **mischief** every time they visit.
4. There's a fish and tackle shop at the end of the **pier.**
5. The **freight** train moved slowly down the tracks.
6. My family bought a **foreign** car.
7. I didn't **receive** my allowance this week.
8. He was pleased to be the **receiver** of an award at the spelling bee.
9. Her mother respected Wendy's **belief** in Peter Pan.
10. The hikers sighed with **relief** as they reached the summit.
11. The grocer **weighed** the plums.
12. Pull back on the **reins,** and the horse will slow down.

(continued on next page)

Pretest

Administer the test on this page as a pretest. Say each word, use it in the sentence, and then repeat the word. ACCESSING PRIOR KNOWLEDGE

SELF-CHECK Have students check their own pretests against the list of Spelling Words. Remind students to write misspelled words in their Lesson Word Logs. STUDENT SELF-ASSESSMENT

Introducing the Lesson

Option A (Open Sort)

Distribute the word cards (page 104) to individuals or small groups, and guide them in an open-sort activity. In open sort, students group the word cards according to a criterion they select themselves. Then guide students in comparing and discussing the criteria they selected.

Option B (Modeling)

Read aloud with students the lesson title and the Spelling Words. Use this model sentence to introduce the lesson skill in a context.

*My dad said I could invite **eight friends.***

Teaching the Lesson

- Have students name Spelling Words that have the vowel combination *ie*, and list them on the board under that heading. Have a volunteer read aloud the words in which *ie* spells the long *e* sound. Follow the same procedure with the other vowel sounds. *(**long e sound:** belief, relief, thieves, achieve; **short e sound:** boyfriend, girlfriend; **short i sound:** mischief, pier, fierce)*
- Have students name Spelling Words that have the vowel combination *ei*. As students name words, list them on the board under the heading "*ei* spells the long *a* sound." Follow the same procedure with the other vowel sounds. *(**long a sound:** freight, weighed, reins; **long e sound:** receive, receiver; **short i sound:** foreign; **long i sound:** heights)*

IN SUMMARY You may want students to summarize the lesson in their own words. Elicit from students that the letter combinations *ei* and *ie* can spell several different vowel sounds.

ASSIGNMENT Students can complete the first page of the lesson as a follow-up to the group activity, either in class or as homework.

Lesson 7: Words with *ie* and *ei* *(continued)*

Practicing the Lesson

Spelling Clues: Letter Patterns

You might like to share this generalization with students: Use *i* before *e* except after *c* or when the sound is long *a* as in *neighbor* or *weigh*. As with any generalization, there are exceptions (for example, *weird*, *seize*, *foreign*, *heights*). Help students identify this lesson's Spelling Words that cause them the most difficulty. Have them print these Spelling Words neatly on index cards or small pieces of paper. Provide time each day for students to look at their cards and to spell each word to themselves as they read it. After they have spelled a word while looking at it, have them close their eyes and visualize the word. Tell them to see the letter pattern in their minds and then to open their eyes and check to see whether they visualized it correctly. Have them do this each day until they have mastered all the words on their individual lists. APPLYING SPELLING STRATEGIES

Proofreading

You may wish to have students review Spelling Clues: Letter Patterns before proofreading the paragraph.

Fun with Words

Have students complete this activity individually. Tell students to use Spelling Words they have not already written on lines 1–12. To extend the activity, you might have students write clues for other Spelling Words.

Posttest

Administer the test on page 14 as a posttest, or administer one of your own. Say each word, use it in a sentence, and then repeat the word.

Reteaching the Lesson

Have students write each Spelling Word on an index card, using one color of marker for the letters *ie*, a second color for the letters *ei*, and a third color for the rest of the letters in each word. Have students work with a partner to practice spelling these words. Have one student select a card at random, read the word aloud, and then ask his or her partner to spell it. If the partner spells the word correctly, the card is placed in a discard pile. If the partner misspells the word, she or he reads the word aloud, spells it while looking at it, and then puts it back in the first pile of cards to be tried again. Have pairs continue until the partner has spelled all the words correctly, then reverse roles. VISUAL/AUDITORY MODALITIES

(Pretest/Posttest, continued)

13. The kitten tried to look **fierce.**

14. Mara is afraid of **heights.**

15. The police arrested the **thieves** and put them in jail.

16. Woody wants to **achieve** a great deal in his life.

PRACTICE ACTIVITY

The practice activity is on page 106.

Answers: Spelling Clues

1. achieve
2. receive
3. relief
4. receiver
5. foreign

Answers: Proofreading

6. heights
7. fierce
8. thieves
9. pier
10. reins
11. freight
12. belief

Answers: Fun with Words

13. mischief
14. weighed
15. boyfriend
16. girlfriend

Lesson 8: Compound Words

OBJECTIVE

To spell open, hyphenated, and closed compound words

HOME ACTIVITY

The home activity is on page 108.

SECOND-LANGUAGE SUPPORT

Explain that compound words do not always mean exactly what they seem to mean. For example, a *greenhouse* is not green. On the other hand, the words combined often give clues to the meaning of the compound word. (A *greenhouse* is a structure, or "house," where green plants are grown.) Moreover, some compound words do mean exactly what they appear to mean. To go *barefoot* is to have bare feet. Have students copy the Spelling Words onto a separate sheet of paper and guess the meanings of the words. Verify or correct their guesses. INFERRING MEANING

PRETEST/POSTTEST

1. The seeds will sprout in the **greenhouse.**
2. Brenda found some shells at the **seashore.**
3. We watched **fireworks** on the Fourth of July.
4. All our club members are **fun-loving.**
5. We rattled cans and shouted Happy **New Year**!
6. "The Ugly Duckling" is one of my favorite **fairy tales.**
7. My mother always reads to me at **bedtime.**
8. The pancake mix is in the **cupboard.**
9. Ben was an **upright** young man who never lied.
10. When you turn thirteen, you become a **teenager.**

(continued on next page)

Pretest

Administer the test on this page as a pretest. Say each word, use it in the sentence, and then repeat the word. ACCESSING PRIOR KNOWLEDGE

SELF-CHECK Have students check their own pretests against the list of Spelling Words. Remind students to write misspelled words in their Lesson Word Logs. STUDENT SELF-ASSESSMENT

Introducing the Lesson

Option A (Open Sort)

Distribute the word cards (page 107) to individuals or small groups, and guide them in an open-sort activity. In open sort, students group the word cards according to a criterion they select themselves. Then, guide students in comparing and discussing the criteria they selected.

Option B (Modeling)

Read aloud with students the lesson title and the Spelling Words. Use this model sentence to introduce the lesson skill.

*My brother built a **make-believe** castle out of **cardboard.***

Teaching the Lesson

- Have students name Spelling Words that are written like *sea horse*. Have a volunteer explain what is the same about these words. (Each is a compound word written as two words.) *(fairy tales, New Year)*
- Have volunteers name Spelling Words that are written like *sea-lane*. Ask what is the same about all these words. (Each is written as a hyphenated word.) *(fun-loving, mean-spirited, middle-aged, so-called)*
- Have students name Spelling Words that are written like the compound word *seagoing*. As students name words, list them on the board. Have a volunteer explain what is the same about all the words in the list. (Each is composed of two words, written as one word.) *(greenhouse, seashore, fireworks, bedtime, cupboard, upright, teenager, thunderstorm, barefoot, bodyguard)*

IN SUMMARY You may want students to summarize the lesson in their own words. Elicit from students that some compound words are written as two words, some as a hyphenated word, and some as one word.

ASSIGNMENT Students can complete the first page of the lesson as a follow-up activity, either in class or as homework.

Lesson 8: Compound Words *(continued)*

Practicing the Lesson

Spelling Clues: Checking Compound Words

Write the following words on the board:

after	any	cream	cube
cut	else	ice	move
noon	one	out	side
some	thing	twenty	where

Call on volunteers to create compound words from the smaller words on the board. Ask students to verify spellings of the words, referring to a dictionary if necessary. When several compound words have been written and their spellings checked, ask students whether the spellings of the smaller words changed when compound words were formed. Tell them that when compound words are created, the spellings of the smaller words from which they are made do not change. APPLYING SPELLING STRATEGIES

TRANSITIONAL SPELLERS Have students draw a line between the two parts of the compound word before they check its spelling. Tell them to check the spelling of each part of the word.

Proofreading

You may wish to have students review Spelling Clues: Checking Compound Words before proofreading the journal entry.

Fun with Words

Have students complete this activity, using Spelling Words they have not written on lines 1–12. Students might enjoy making up clues for other compound words and then exchanging papers and having a classmate write the Spelling Words that match the clues.

Posttest

Administer the test on page 16 as a posttest, or administer one of your own. Say each word, use it in a sentence, and then repeat the word.

Reteaching the Lesson

Do this activity in groups of three to five students. Distribute index cards or slips of paper to each person. Assign three to five of the compound words to each student, and have students write each part of their compound words on a separate card. Put all the cards in a pile. Then, in a round-robin fashion, have each student find in the pile two words that together make a Spelling Word. VISUAL/KINESTHETIC MODALITIES

(Pretest/Posttest, continued)

11. The **thunderstorm** knocked out the electric power.
12. The children ran **barefoot** across the sand.
13. They live in a **middle-class** neighborhood.
14. Joan is **mean-spirited** and often makes fun of other students.
15. Many famous people employ a **bodyguard.**
16. Sherlock Holmes and his **so-called** assistant caught the thieves.

PRACTICE ACTIVITY

The practice activity is on page 109.

Answers: Spelling Clues

1. bodyguard
2. upright
3. New Year
4. thunderstorm
5. mean-spirited
6. so-called

Answers: Proofreading

7. fun-loving
8. teenager
9. seashore
10. bedtime
11. middle-aged
12. fireworks

Answers: Fun with Words

13. barefoot
14. fairy tales
15. cupboard
16. greenhouse

Lesson 9: Homophones

OBJECTIVE
To spell homophones

HOME ACTIVITY
The home activity is on page 111.

SECOND-LANGUAGE SUPPORT
Tell students that in English there are words that sound exactly alike but that are spelled differently and have different meanings. These words are called *homophones*. Make the difference concrete by putting pictures of some of the words on cards. Below each picture, write the correct spelling. You might use *steak* and *stake* since they are easy to illustrate. After drawing students' attention to the two spellings, provide sentences with blanks, and have students insert the right homophone in each. Extend the exercise by having students make similar cards for other homophones. USING PICTURE CLUES

PRETEST/POSTTEST
1. There are seven days in a **week.**
2. He was as **weak** as a kitten.
3. The bridge's girders are made out of **steel.**
4. The robbers planned to **steal** a painting.
5. My plant has **grown** some new leaves.
6. Did the fans **groan** when the shortstop made an error?
7. My grandparents say that I am their special **guest.**
8. We **guessed** at the spelling of the French words.
9. If the **creek** rises, it will flood our fields.
10. Did you hear a door **creak**?
11. Mr. Chang is hoping for sunnier **weather.**
12. Do you know **whether** Ryan is coming or not?

(continued on next page)

Pretest
Administer the test on this page as a pretest. Say each word, use it in the sentence, and then repeat the word. ACCESSING PRIOR KNOWLEDGE

Self-Check Have students check their own pretests against the list of Spelling Words. Remind students to write misspelled words in their Lesson Word Logs. STUDENT SELF-ASSESSMENT

Introducing the Lesson

Option A (Open Sort)
Distribute the word cards (page 110) to individuals or small groups, and guide them in an open-sort activity. In open sort, students group the word cards according to a criterion they select themselves. Then, guide students in comparing and discussing the criteria they selected.

Option B (Modeling)
Read aloud with students the lesson title and the Spelling Words. Use this model sentence to introduce the lesson skill in a context.

*I can **hear** her whispering from way over **here.***

Teaching the Lesson
- Have volunteers write the homophones on the board side by side. *(week/weak; steel/steal; grown/groan; guest/guessed; creek/creak; sore/soar; stake/steak; weather/whether)*
- One at a time, have volunteers choose a pair, use each homophone in a sentence, and spell the homophone after each sentence. You might want to point out that *weather* and *whether* are often referred to as near homophones because the *w* and *wh* sounds are not actually identical.
- After students have added pairs of homophones from their own reading or writing, have each student read his or her pairs and use each word in a sentence.

In Summary You may want students to summarize the lesson in their own words. Elicit from students that homophones are words that sound the same but have different spellings and different meanings.

Assignment Students can complete the first page of the lesson as a follow-up to the group activity, either in class or as homework.

Lesson 9: Homophones *(continued)*

Practicing the Lesson

Spelling Clues: Spelling and Meaning

Have students look at the words *guessed* and *guest*. Elicit the meaning of *guessed* (past tense of *guess*). Underline the word *guess* in *guessed*. Explain that seeing the word *guess* in *guessed* tells them which homophone to use in a sentence like this: "I _____ the right answer." Tell them that thinking about meaning helps in choosing the right homophone.

Explain that homophones should always be used in context; otherwise there is no way to determine the correct spelling. Encourage students to check a dictionary when they are unsure of which homophone to use. APPLYING SPELLING STRATEGIES

Proofreading

You may wish to have students review Spelling Clues: Spelling and Meaning before proofreading the sentences.

Working with Meaning

Students who need an additional challenge might enjoy writing sentences using three-to-a-group homophones like *right, write, rite; borough, burro, burrow; there, they're, their;* and *I, aye, eye.*

Posttest

Administer the test on page 18 as a posttest, or administer one of your own. Say each word, use it in a sentence, and then repeat the word.

Reteaching the Lesson

This game works well in a circle. Begin by displaying the Spelling Words in pairs. To begin, a student chooses a pair of homophones without telling the others what pair was selected. The student gives a clue to the person sitting on her or his left, and that student has to guess the homophone.

For example, the student might say, "Just change an *e* for an *a*, and it rhymes with *meek.*" If the second student guesses the pair *creek/creak* or the pair *week/weak*, he or she gets a point. Then that student gives a clue, such as this: "Drop three letters and add a *t*." If the next student answers *guessed/guest*, he or she gets a point, and so on.

Keep going until each student has had two or three chances to think up clues and to guess the correct pair. The player with the most points wins. AUDITORY MODALITY

(Pretest/Posttest, continued)

13. The dry air makes my lips **sore.**
14. I saw a buzzard **soar** out of the cornfields.
15. My cucumbers are climbing up the **stake** I put in the ground.
16. Do you want fish or **steak** for dinner?

PRACTICE ACTIVITY

The practice activity is on page 112.

Answers: Spelling Clues

1. steal
2. steel
3. steak
4. stake

Answers: Proofreading

5. guessed
6. week
7. weak
8. guest
9. groan
10. grown

Answers: Working with Meaning

11. whether
12. weather
13. soar
14. sore
15. creak
16. creek

Lesson 10: Easily Confused Words

OBJECTIVE
To spell words that sound similar and have spellings that are somewhat alike

HOME ACTIVITY
The home activity is on page 114.

SECOND-LANGUAGE SUPPORT
Ask students for examples of words in their other language that can be easily confused. For example, in Spanish, the words *nuevo (new), nueve (nine),* and *nieve (snow)* might be confused. Then, write the Spelling Words, two at a time, on the board. Pronounce each word carefully, placing special emphasis on the parts of the word that can be easily confused. As you say each word, have students repeat the word after you. Provide a simple definition of the word. Then, as you point to each letter, have students spell the word aloud with you. COMPARING AND CONTRASTING

PRETEST/POSTTEST
1. I'll wash the car **later.**
2. When he asked me if I wanted a muffin or bagel, I said the **latter.**
3. Amy won't eat any vegetables **except** corn.
4. Fran wouldn't **accept** any money for baby-sitting.
5. My math teacher said to draw the line at a 45° **angle.**
6. In art class, we learned how to make an **angel** with see-through wings.
7. My **costume** for the play doesn't fit well.
8. I enjoy the **custom** of having a children's table at big family gatherings.
9. Seeing the movie again didn't **affect** my feelings about it.

(continued on next page)

Pretest
Administer the test on this page as a pretest. Say each word, use it in the sentence, and then repeat the word. ACCESSING PRIOR KNOWLEDGE

Self-Check Have students check their own pretests against the list of Spelling Words. Remind students to write misspelled words in their Lesson Word Logs. STUDENT SELF-ASSESSMENT

Introducing the Lesson

Option A (Open Sort)
Distribute the word cards (page 113) to individuals or small groups, and guide them in an open-sort activity. In open sort, students group the word cards according to a criterion they select themselves. Then, guide students in comparing and discussing the criteria they selected.

Option B (Modeling)
Read aloud with students the lesson title and the Spelling Words. Use this model sentence to introduce the lesson skill in a context.

*She could **accept** all the excuses **except** mine!*

Teaching the Lesson
- Have volunteers find words with the accent on the first syllable. Write each word on the board, side by side with its easily confused counterpart. (Note that *decent* is accented on the first syllable, whereas *descent* is accented on the second syllable.) *(later/latter; angle/angel; costume/custom; decent/descent)*
- Follow the same procedure with words that have the accent on the second syllable. *(except/accept; affect/effect; adopt/adapt; device/devise; descent/decent)*
- After students have added to the columns pairs of easily confused words from their own reading or writing, have volunteers choose word pairs and use each word in a sentence.

In Summary You may want students to summarize the lesson in their own words. Elicit from them that some words sound a lot like other words but actually have different pronunciations, spellings, and meanings.

Assignment Students can complete the first page of the lesson as a follow-up to the group activity, either in class or as homework.

Lesson 10: Easily Confused Words *(continued)*

Practicing the Lesson

Spelling Clues: Using Definitions

Suggest that when students are not sure whether they are using the correct word, they should consult a dictionary to see whether that is the word they meant to use. Remind them that even adults have to check word meanings and spellings occasionally. Words like *affect* and *effect* that are close in meaning as well as in pronunciation and spelling are especially tricky. Remind students that they may need to look them up several times to be sure they are using the correct word. Tell students never to be hesitant to use a dictionary. Remind them that the more they use a word incorrectly, the more acceptable it will seem, and the harder it will be to learn correct usage later. APPLYING SPELLING STRATEGIES

TRANSITIONAL SPELLERS Write the Spelling Words in pairs on the board. Read aloud a short definition of each word, and have students choose the word that matches the definition and write the word on one side of a flashcard. Check for accuracy. Then, have them write the definition on the other side of the flashcard as you dictate it. Try to provide time each day for students to study their flashcards.

Proofreading

You may wish to have students review Spelling Clues: Using Definitions before proofreading the article.

Working with Meaning

Have students replace the numbers in the cartoons with Spelling Words they have not written on lines 1–12.

Posttest

Administer the test on page 20 as a posttest, or administer one of your own. Say each word, use it in a sentence, and then repeat the word.

Reteaching the Lesson

Have a volunteer write the Spelling Words in pairs on the board. Read aloud a short definition of each word, and have students select and write on one side of a flashcard the word that matches the definition. Check for accuracy. Then, have students write the definition on the other side as you dictate it. Provide time for students to study their flashcards with a partner. KINESTHETIC MODALITY

(Pretest/Posttest, continued)

10. Sometimes understanding has a better **effect** on people than punishment.

11. Did Devin's parents **adopt** another child?

12. I will **adapt** to the changes in the schedule.

13. I wish I had a **device** that would automatically empty trash cans.

14. The prisoners could not **devise** a means of escape.

15. My parents expect me to wear **decent** clothes to school.

16. Their **descent** into the canyon was full of surprises.

PRACTICE ACTIVITY

The practice activity is on page 115.

Answers: Spelling Clues

1. devise
2. latter
3. affect
4. descent
5. device
6. angle

Answers: Proofreading

7. custom
8. accept
9. costume
10. effect
11. except
12. later

Answers: Working with Meaning

13. adopt
14. angel
15. adapt
16. decent

Unit 2 Review

OBJECTIVES

- To review spelling patterns and strategies in Lessons 6–10
- To give students the opportunity to recognize and use these spelling patterns and Spelling Words in their writing

UNIT 2 WORDS

The following words are reviewed in Practice Test, Parts A and B.

Lesson 6: Other Vowel Spellings

biscuit straight
dough courage

Lesson 7: Words with *ie* and *ei*

fierce receive
freight

Lesson 8: Compound Words

bedtime thunderstorm
middle-aged

Lesson 9: Homophones

grown steel
creak weak
guessed

Lesson 10: Easily Confused Words

adopt angle
later decent
affect

Review Strategies

Review with students the following spelling-clue strategies for Lessons 6–10.

Lesson 6 Spelling Clues: Word Shapes

Write the word *although* on the board. Ask students to identify the letters in the word that reach above the midline *(l, t, h, h).* Then, have them identify the letter that hangs below the baseline *(g).* Remind students that noting the shapes of letters can sometimes help them remember how to spell words.

Lesson 7 Spelling Clues: Letter Patterns

Have students close their eyes. Then, say the word *achieve* aloud. Ask students to picture the word in their mind. What is the pattern of letters—especially the pattern of the *i* and the *e*? Tell students to write the word on paper as they see the word in their mind. Then have them put responses on the board (*acheive* and *achieve,* for example), and determine which is correct. Explain that visualizing letter patterns can help them spell a word.

Lesson 8 Spelling Clues: Checking Compound Words

Write *thundorstorm* on the board. Ask students what two words they recognize in this compound. Have them identify the word that is misspelled *(thundor)* and give the correct spelling *(thunder).* Point out that it is helpful to break down a compound word into its smaller words when checking its spelling.

Lesson 9 Spelling Clues: Spelling and Meaning

Say the word *steal* aloud. Ask students to name two possible ways of spelling the word *(steal, steel).* Then say, "It's against the law to steal." Have students tell which spelling belongs in the sentence, and then have them give an example of a sentence using *steel.* Point out that when students are spelling homophones, they should keep in mind the meaning of the intended word.

Lesson 10 Spelling Clues: Using Definitions

Write the words *latter* and *later* on the board. Ask students how the words are similar and why they might easily be confused. Invite volunteers to say each word and use it in a sentence. Point out that when students are spelling a word easily confused with another word, they should keep in mind the meaning of the intended word.

Unit 2 Review *(continued)*

Practice Test

The Practice Test provides an opportunity to review Spelling Words and spelling generalizations in a standardized test format, complete with a sample answer card.

Option 1

Use Practice Test: Part A as a pretest. Later, use Practice Test: Part B as a posttest.

Option 2

Have students review their Lesson Word Log for this unit. If they need extra help, you may wish to review the spelling generalizations discussed in the individual lessons. Then administer both parts of the Practice Test to determine whether students have mastered the spelling generalizations.

Practice Test: Part A

1. incorrect [biscuit]
2. correct [dough]
3. incorrect [grown]
4. incorrect [straight]
5. correct [fierce]
6. incorrect [adopt]
7. incorrect [freight]
8. incorrect [bedtime]
9. incorrect [middle-aged]
10. correct [creak]

Practice Test: Part B

1. (C) guessed
2. (A) steel
3. (A) weak
4. (D) thunderstorm
5. (C) courage
6. (B) later
7. (A) affect
8. (B) angle
9. (C) decent
10. (D) receive

Options for Evaluation

- Have students check their own Practice Tests against their lists of Spelling Words. The list on the opposite page provides references to the lessons where they can find words they misspelled.
- You may prefer to assign partners and have students check each other's Practice Tests, using their own list of Spelling Words.

REVIEW ACTIVITIES

Activity 1

Prepare paper plates, each with a different letter of the alphabet on it. Distribute one plate to each student, adjusting as needed for the number of students in the class. Say aloud a word from this review lesson, and have students who are holding the letters in that word line up to spell the word. If a letter appears more than once in a word (as the *e* in *fierce*, for example), the student holding that letter must then move between other students to indicate where the letter is repeated.

Activity 2

Have students play a game called "Blank!" After you have organized small groups, let one player in each group choose a word from this review lesson and make up a sentence using that word, but saying the word *blank* in place of the word—for example: "Baseball season is now, but football season comes *blank*." (The word is *later*.) Group members then try to guess the "blank" word. At the end of the round, another group member chooses a different word and follows the same procedure.

Activity 3

Use the words from this review lesson to play this game. Set a time period, such as two minutes. Have students write a phrase for each word in the lesson (for example, "*bedtime* story" or "*freight* train"). The writing must be neat enough so that the Spelling Words can be read clearly. Later, let students share their phrases with a partner, who can check the first student's list for correct spelling.

Unit 2 Review *(continued)*

WHAT'S IN A WORD?

catalpa

You might want to have students name other plants that carry a symbolic meaning. For example, a *red rose* connotes love to many people; the *oak* symbolizes great strength; and the *bluebonnet* (a wild lupine also known as *el conejo* or buffalo clover) carries the meaning of forgiveness or sacrifice.

courage

Students might enjoy listing expressions with the word *heart* in them. You might begin by telling students that throughout the ages, many cultures have considered the heart to be the center of emotions. For example, a Mexican girl might refer to her favorite brother as *mi hermanito de mi corazón* ("my brother of my heart"). In English, we say a sad person is *heartbroken*. Have students see how many other "heart expressions" they can list.

♦ cupboard

Have students research the history of other common compound words, such as *handkerchief, taxicab, baseball,* and *soda pop*. You might have them compare the original meaning with that of today's meaning.

♦ This indicates a Unit Spelling Word.

Unit Activity Options

Checking Up

You may want to have students choose four or five meanings that are new to them and have them write sample sentences using their Spelling Words in this new way.

Synonym Spell-Check

After students have had an opportunity to complete the Synonym Spell-Check activity with a partner, collect the synonyms and use them to review all the Spelling Words. Having more than one synonym for a Spelling Word will give students more than one chance to review each Spelling Word.

Proofreading Partners

Encourage partners to discuss their ideas for paragraphs. Remind them that, to include the listed words, they may need to create an unusual or even a fantastic situation in their paragraphs.

Tongue Twisters

Write a few of the best tongue twisters on the board, and let students vote for the twister that tangles the most tongues.

Homophone Fun

Remind students to be sure that they have given adequate context clues so that a classmate can identify the pair of homophones.

Secret Messages

Review the activity instructions with students. Have several volunteers suggest appropriate secret messages and identify the abbreviations they would use in writing those messages. Then have students choose their own partners and encode their secret messages. You may want to suggest that students use at least one Spelling Word in each message.

Antonym Spelling

You may want to have students write the Spelling Words in one column and the antonym for each word in another column.

WORKING TOGETHER For the Antonym Spelling activity, allow time for pairs of students to play the game.

Unit 2 Review *(continued)*

Curriculum Options

Cross-Curriculum: In a Class by Yourself

Organize students into several groups. Tell them that in this game every group can win if the members try hard enough. The object of the game is to list as many compound words as they can for the subject area you assign to them. Their group wins if they list at least twenty words. Remind students that compound words may be written as one word, may be hyphenated, or may be written as two words. Allow them to consult any books you have in the classroom to help them find words.

Language Arts: Spelling Password

This game is played with four students, two on each team. A fifth student is the host. Select a visual learner as the host. The host has sixteen cards with a Spelling Word written on each card. The host gives a card to one of the players on Team A without letting the other players see the word. That player offers a one-word clue to the word. Some Spelling Words and their one-word clues might be *second* (latter), *play* (costume), *change* (adapt), *tradition* (custom), and *borrow* (adopt).

If the player's teammate guesses the word and spells it correctly, Team A gets a point. If the wrong word is guessed, a player from Team B looks at the card and gives his or her teammate a different one-word clue for the word. If the teammate guesses the word and spells it correctly, Team B gets the point. If the guess is wrong, Team A gets another turn, and so on. Teams take turns starting each new word.

Social Studies: In the News

Students will need to prepare for this game by creating questions that can be answered by a Spelling Word. Questions can be based on local or national events. The game is played in two teams of three or four persons per team. Team A begins by asking Team B a question. If a member of Team B answers it correctly and spells the Spelling Word correctly, Team B gets two points. If the answer is wrong, but the word is spelled correctly, the team gets one point. (You may want to make up a rule about players taking turns answering questions so that one student doesn't answer them all for his or her team.) Teams should take turns asking questions. The team with more points wins.

WHAT'S IN A WORD?

giraffe

You may want to share the following list of animal names.

prairie dog	groundhog
bobcat	box turtle
muskrat	guinea pig
mongoose	kangaroo rat
wolf spider	panda bear
wombat	elephant seal

Have students sort them into two categories: names that tell what kind of animal something really is and names that don't.

heroine

Students may be interested to learn that the character Hero in the Greek tale was female, lending some support to the notion of using the word *hero* to refer to both males and females. Point out to students that reading and remembering Greek tales can help them unlock the meanings of many English words.

Working Together Students may enjoy listing male and female forms of words, such as *fireman* and *policewoman*, and discussing possible nonsexist replacements. *(firefighter, police officer)*

spectator

You might want to review the difference between *denotation* and *connotation*. Discuss with students the differences between the words *spectator, seer, watcher, observer, onlooker, gazer,* and *rubbernecker*. Tell them that a word choice often does more than give facts; it often displays an attitude and nudges the reader toward a point of view.

TEACHING STRATEGIES

Lesson 12: Changing *y* to *i*

OBJECTIVE

To spell words ending with consonant -*y* in which *y* changes to *i* before -*es* or -*ed* is added

HOME ACTIVITY

The home activity is on page 117.

SECOND-LANGUAGE SUPPORT

Often, students with limited English proficiency omit the -*es* required by *he* or *she*, forming sentences such as "She try hard in school." Have students brainstorm verbs ending with consonant -*y*, such as *fly*, *dry*, and *apply*, and write the words on the board. Then, have a volunteer recite a sentence starting with *he* or *she* that uses one of the verbs. Write the sentence on the board and point out the -*es* ending. SUBJECT-VERB AGREEMENT

PRETEST/ POSTTEST

1. A state may have hundreds of towns and **cities** in it.
2. In Egypt long ago, **mummies** were buried in tombs.
3. The workers brought the **supplies** they needed.
4. Several **families** lived in the area.
5. The **varied** menu in the cafeteria appealed to my friends and me.
6. The car was invented less than two **centuries** ago.
7. Many **colonies** began to grow as people tried to make new lives.
8. Jane **applies** cream to her face each day.
9. The baby **occupied** herself with a spoon and a plastic dish.
10. Sam **identified** the person who had pushed him.
11. The **enemies** decided to stop their fighting.
12. What **activities** did you do at summer camp?
13. The man **denied** the charges made against him.

(continued on next page)

Pretest

Administer the test on this page as a pretest. Say each word, use it in the sentence, and then repeat the word. ACCESSING PRIOR KNOWLEDGE

SELF-CHECK Have students check their own pretests against the list of Spelling Words. Remind students to write misspelled words in their Lesson Word Logs. STUDENT SELF-ASSESSMENT

Introducing the Lesson

Option A (Open Sort)

Distribute the word cards (page 116) to individuals or small groups, and guide them in an open-sort activity. In open sort, students group the word cards according to a criterion they select themselves. Then, guide students in comparing and discussing the criteria they selected.

Option B (Modeling)

Read aloud with students the lesson title and the Spelling Words. Use this model sentence to introduce the lesson skill in a context.

*I **tried** to count all the **pennies**.*

Teaching the Lesson

- Ask volunteers to name some Spelling Words that come from base words ending with consonant -*y*. After listing the words, have volunteers go to the board, change *y* to *i*, and then add -*es*. *(cities, mummies, supplies, families, centuries, colonies, applies, enemies, activities, industries)*
- Follow the same procedure with other consonant -*y* words. Have volunteers go to the board, change *y* to *i*, and then add -*ed*. *(varied, occupied, identified, denied, allied, qualified)*
- After students add words from their own writing to the board, have all the words read aloud and the -*ies* or -*ied* spelling at the end of each word underlined.

IN SUMMARY You may want students to summarize the lesson in their own words. Elicit from students that knowing the rule for changing *y* to *i* can help them spell other consonant -*y* words when an -*es* or -*ed* ending is required.

ASSIGNMENT Students can complete the first page of the lesson as a follow-up to the group activity, either in class or as homework.

Lesson 12: Changing *y* to *i* *(continued)*

Practicing the Lesson

Spelling Clues: Spelling Rules

Suggest that when students apply the spelling rule in this lesson, they should first check that the original word indeed ends with consonant *-y*. Remind students that a word ending with vowel *-y* , such as *monkey*, does not follow the same rule. APPLYING SPELLING STRATEGIES

TRANSITIONAL SPELLERS Have students complete this activity with a partner or in a small group.

Proofreading

You may wish to have students review Spelling Clues: Spelling Rules before proofreading the note.

Working with Meaning

Students may complete this activity independently or with a partner. Tell them to use Spelling Words they have not already used on lines 1–12. Ask students what they notice about the ending of all the words they used. (They all have *-ed* endings.) The Spelling Dictionary can be used to check definitions.

SECOND-LANGUAGE SUPPORT Have students work with a partner, each reading one character's dialogue from the cartoon. Let each student explain the meaning of the dialogue. USING CONTEXT CLUES

Posttest

Administer the test on page 26 as a posttest, or administer one of your own. Say each word, use it in a sentence, and then repeat the word.

Reteaching the Lesson

On a set of index cards, write each Spelling Word as it would be spelled before the *-es* or *-ed* ending is added. On another set of index cards, write each Spelling Word as it appears with the *-es* or *-ed* ending.

city cities

Have students randomly draw a card from the first group and read the word aloud. Then have them find the corresponding card from the second group that shows the word with its ending. Have students write the first word on the board. Then have them cross out the final *y* and add *-es* or *-ed*. Finally, have them write the Spelling Word again with its proper ending. KINESTHETIC MODALITY

(Pretest/Posttest, continued)

14. France **allied** itself with Spain during the war.
15. Many new **industries** have opened in our town.
16. Who is most **qualified** for the job?

PRACTICE ACTIVITY

The practice activity is on page 118.

Answers: Spelling Clues

1. supplies
2. enemies
3. allies
4. industries
5. colonies
6. applies

Answers: Proofreading

7. occupied
8. activities
9. centuries
10. mummies
11. families
12. cities

Answers: Working with Meaning

13. identified
14. denied
15. varied
16. qualified

Lesson 13: Endings /ər/, /əl/, /ən/

OBJECTIVE

To spell words that demonstrate these sound-letter relationships: /ər/*er;* /əl/ *al;* /ən/*an, en*

HOME ACTIVITY

The home activity is on page 120.

SECOND-LANGUAGE SUPPORT

The /əl/ sound at the end of a word may cause difficulty for students whose native language is Chinese, Japanese, Korean, Vietnamese, or Thai. They may confuse the /əl/ sound with the /ər/ sound. Have students think of words they know ending in /əl/ or /ər/. Write each word on the board. Have volunteers say each word aloud, stressing its ending sound and underlining the letters that spell the sound. COMPARING AND CONTRASTING

PRETEST/POSTTEST

1. The eager **reader** visited the library often.
2. Who will be the **speaker** at our next meeting?
3. The builders added another **layer** of bricks.
4. Baseball is a popular **American** sport.
5. The team was **beaten** by only one point.
6. Which **musical** instrument is your favorite?
7. This old apple has become **rotten.**
8. Hot dogs were first a **German** treat.
9. Gandhi was a great **Indian** leader.
10. The **Roman** army won many battles.
11. That **explorer** took many risks.
12. They carried the man out on a **stretcher.**

(continued on next page)

Pretest

Administer the test on this page as a pretest. Say each word, use it in the sentence, and then repeat the word. ACCESSING PRIOR KNOWLEDGE

SELF-CHECK Have students check their own pretests against the list of Spelling Words. Remind students to write misspelled words in their Lesson Word Logs. STUDENT SELF-ASSESSMENT

Introducing the Lesson

Option A (Open Sort)

Distribute the word cards (page 119) to individuals or small groups, and guide them in an open-sort activity. In open sort, students group the word cards according to a criterion they select themselves. Then guide students in comparing and discussing the criteria they selected.

Option B (Modeling)

Read aloud with students the lesson title and the Spelling Words. Use this model sentence to introduce the lesson skill in a context.

*The **singer** has **forgotten** the words.*

Teaching the Lesson

- Ask volunteers to name some words that have the same ending sound they hear in *butter*. As students name words, list them on the board. After students have named words, have them identify those words in which the /ər/ sound is spelled *er*. *(reader, speaker, layer, explorer, stretcher)*
- Follow the same procedure for words ending in /əl/ and /ən/. Have students identify those /ən/ words ending with *-an* or *-en*. (**/əl/:** *critical, criminal, political, original, musical;* **/ən/:** *American, beaten, rotten, German, Indian, Roman)*
- After students have added words from their own writing to the columns, have all the words read aloud and the spelling of each ending schwa sound underlined.

IN SUMMARY You may want students to summarize the lesson in their own words. Elicit from students that /ər/ is usually spelled *er*, /əl/ is often spelled *al*, and /ən/ is usually spelled *an* or *en*.

ASSESSMENT Students can complete the first page of the lesson as a follow-up to the group activity, either in class or as homework.

Lesson 13: Endings /ər/, /əl/, /ən/ *(continued)*

Practicing the Lesson

Spelling Clues: Best-Guess Spelling

Suggest that before students write their "best guess," they close their eyes and try to envision the letters in their mind. Then they should write the spelling the way they "see" it.

Point out that the spelling patterns in this lesson can help students make a best guess. For example, most /ər/ words are spelled *er*, as opposed to other possible spellings such as *or* or *ar*. Likewise, many /əl/ words are spelled *al*, as opposed to other possible spellings such as *il* or *le*. Students should try the spellings given in this lesson as their best guess and then try another spelling only if the first guess doesn't look correct. APPLYING SPELLING STRATEGIES

TRANSITIONAL SPELLERS Have students complete the activity with a partner. Each student can check the partner's best guess and then say whether it is right or wrong.

Proofreading

You may wish to have students review Spelling Clues: Best-Guess Spelling before proofreading the note.

Working with Meaning

Students may complete this activity independently or with a partner. Point out that the words they choose should reflect the person's heritage.

SECOND-LANGUAGE SUPPORT Encourage students to explain how the details in each illustration helped them decide on the appropriate word. USING PICTURE CLUES

Posttest

Administer the test on page 28 as a posttest, or administer one of your own. Say each word, use it in a sentence, and then repeat the word.

Reteaching the Lesson

Divide the Spelling Words into lists, one for each unstressed ending. Have students read the Spelling Words appearing in each column. Let them say each word aloud, stressing the schwa-consonant sound at the end of the word. Students should spell each word aloud, stressing the letters that spell the schwa-consonant ending sound. Then have students write each word and say the letters aloud as they write. AUDITORY MODALITY

(Pretest/Posttest, continued)

13. I must make a **critical** choice.

14. The **criminal** spent five years in jail.

15. To which **political** party does he belong?

16. The **original** page was used to make a copy.

PRACTICE ACTIVITY

The practice activity is on page 121.

Answers: Spelling Clues

1. American	**4.** German
2. political	**5.** criminal
3. reader	**6.** explorer

Answers: Proofreading

7. rotten	**10.** critical
8. original	**11.** stretcher
9. beaten	**12.** layer

Answers: Working with Meaning

13. Roman	**15.** speaker
14. Indian	**16.** musical

Lesson 14: Patterns—VC/CV Words

OBJECTIVE

To spell two-syllable words that contain a vowel-consonant-consonant-vowel (VC/CV) pattern

HOME ACTIVITY

The home activity is on page 123.

SECOND-LANGUAGE SUPPORT

The first syllable of a two-syllable word having the VC/CV pattern usually has a short vowel sound. Short /a/ may sound like short /e/ to students with limited English proficiency, and they may pronounce short /i/ as long /e/. Have students brainstorm English words they know that have the VC/CV pattern. Write the words on the board, and then have students say each word aloud, stressing the vowel sound in each syllable. COMPARING AND CONTRASTING

PRETEST/POSTTEST

1. The **pillow** was filled with feathers.
2. Bob **indeed** deserved the reward.
3. Some people thought a **monster** lived in the lake.
4. There were **fifteen** people on the bus.
5. The man made his **escape** at night.
6. Have you **gotten** your ticket to the concert yet?
7. Jane wore a **velvet** dress to the party.
8. The car's **engine** wouldn't start during the cold spell.
9. We **insist** that you stay for dinner.
10. I **admire** your talent as an artist.
11. Look in the book's **index** to see where a topic is discussed.
12. The students did some **intense** studying before the exams.
13. The officer questioned the suspect **further.**

(continued on next page)

Pretest

Administer the test on this page as a pretest. Say each word, use it in the sentence, and then repeat the word. ACCESSING PRIOR KNOWLEDGE

SELF-CHECK Have students check their own pretests against the list of Spelling Words. Remind students to write misspelled words in their Lesson Word Logs. STUDENT SELF-ASSESSMENT

Introducing the Lesson

Option A (Open Sort)

Distribute the word cards (page 122) to individuals or small groups, and guide them in an open-sort activity. In open sort, students group the word cards according to a criterion they select themselves. Then guide students in comparing and discussing the criteria they selected.

Option B (Modeling)

Read aloud with students the lesson title and the Spelling Words. Use this model sentence to introduce the lesson skill in a context.

I dropped a ***pencil*** *on the* ***carpet****.*

Teaching the Lesson

- Ask volunteers to name the words that have the same VC/CV pattern that appears in *follow*. List the words on the board. Have students identify the double consonant in the middle of the word. *(pillow, gotten)*
- Follow the same procedure with VC/CV words having two different consonants in the middle, as in *wonder*. *(indeed, fifteen, escape, velvet, engine, insist, admire, index, intense, frantic, convince)*
- Follow the same procedure with VC/CV words having a consonant plus a cluster or digraph. Point out that these words may not look like VC/CV words but that the cluster or digraph functions as one consonant. *(monster, further, instinct)*
- After students add words from their own writing to the columns, have all the words read aloud and the spelling of each VC/CV pattern underlined.

IN SUMMARY You may want students to summarize the lesson in their own words. Elicit from students that the first syllable of a word having a VC/CV pattern usually has a short vowel sound.

ASSIGNMENT Students can complete the first page of the lesson as a follow-up activity, either in class or as homework.

Lesson 14: Patterns—VC/CV Words *(continued)*

Practicing the Lesson

Spelling Clues: Syllabication

Suggest that before students divide a word into syllables, they say the word aloud. Often, hearing where the word "breaks" will help them recognize where to place the hyphen in the word. Remind students that words are not divided between the letters of a cluster or digraph. Write the word *afraid* on the board. Ask students where the syllable break occurs. If they say the break should be between the *f* and the *r*, remind them that the letters *fr* form a consonant cluster. The correct break would therefore have to be before the cluster: *a-fraid*. Encourage students to name other words they know with a cluster or digraph and decide together where each word would be broken into syllables. Have students identify Spelling Words with a cluster or digraph *(monster, further, instinct)*. APPLYING SPELLING STRATEGIES

Proofreading

You may wish to have students review Spelling Clues: Syllabication before proofreading the paragraph.

Fun with Words

Students may complete this activity individually or with a partner. If students need help, tell them that the words in italics have the same spelling endings as the rhyming Spelling Words.

SECOND-LANGUAGE SUPPORT Have students read their sentences aloud to partners. Then have them explain the meaning of each sentence in their own words. USING CONTEXT CLUES

Posttest

Administer the test on page 30 as a posttest, or administer one of your own. Say each word, use it in a sentence, and then repeat the word.

Reteaching the Lesson

Divide the Spelling Words into lists, one for double consonants and one for two different consonants. Students may benefit from learning mnemonic devices that will prompt their recall of syllabication generalizations taught in the lesson. Help them learn that syllables may be divided between two consonants when the consonants are "sandwiched" between the two vowels. Have the students underline the two vowels and two consonants and divide the "sandwich filling" with a line, for example, *pil/low.* VISUAL MODALITY

(Pretest/Posttest, continued)

14. Bill became **frantic** when he couldn't find his keys.
15. How will I **convince** you that I am right?
16. A cat hunts birds by **instinct.**

PRACTICE ACTIVITY

The practice activity is on page 124.

Answers: Spelling Clues

1. fur-ther
2. en-gine
3. fif-teen
4. in-stinct
5. in-deed
6. got-ten

Answers: Proofreading

7. velvet
8. pillow
9. insist
10. admire
11. monster
12. convince
13. escape

Answers: Fun with Words

14. frantic
15. intense
16. index

Lesson 15: Patterns—V/CV Words

OBJECTIVE

To spell two-syllable words that contain a vowel-consonant-vowel (V/CV) pattern

HOME ACTIVITY

The home activity is on page 126.

SECOND-LANGUAGE SUPPORT

In two-syllable words with the V/CV pattern, the first syllable usually has a long vowel sound. Students whose first language is Vietnamese, Spanish, or Tagalog may have difficulty differentiating between the long *a* and short *e* sounds, as in *race* and *pet*. Have students brainstorm two-syllable words with the V/CV pattern. Write the words on the board, and have students underline the V/CV vowel sounds. COMPARING AND CONTRASTING

PRETEST/POSTTEST

1. The game will be played next **Friday.**
2. The cook wore a long white **apron.**
3. What is your **motive** for studying Latin?
4. The runner won the race by one **meter.**
5. The secret **agent** worked as a spy.
6. An **evil** plan was worked out by the villain.
7. Our **local** library has the most books of any library in the state.
8. We are **eager** to see the new movie.
9. Have you ever met anyone **famous**?
10. The doctor said to eat foods that have a lot of **fiber**.
11. Be careful when you use that sharp **razor.**
12. I have some **vital** information you must hear.

(continued on next page)

Pretest

Administer the test on this page as a pretest. Say each word, use it in the sentence, and then repeat the word. ACCESSING PRIOR KNOWLEDGE

SELF-CHECK Have students check their own pretests against the list of Spelling Words. Remind students to write misspelled words in their Lesson Word Logs. STUDENT SELF-ASSESSMENT

Introducing the Lesson

Option A (Open Sort)

Distribute the word cards (page 125) to individuals or small groups, and guide them in an open-sort activity. In open sort, students group the word cards according to a criterion they select themselves. Then guide students in comparing and discussing the criteria they selected.

Option B (Modeling)

Read aloud with students the lesson title and the Spelling Words. Use this model sentence to introduce the lesson skill in a context.

*The **pupils** held a **private** meeting.*

Teaching the Lesson

- Ask volunteers to name the two-syllable Spelling Words that have the V/CV patterns with a long *a* sound in the first syllable, as in *radar*. As students name words, list them on the board. Then have students draw a line to divide each word into syllables. *(apron, agent, famous, razor, basis)*
- Follow the same procedure with V/CV words having a long *e*, *i*, or *o* sound in the first syllable. *(meter, evil, eager, cheetah, scenic, Friday, fiber, vital, rival, motive, local)*
- After students add words from their own writing to the columns, have volunteers read the words aloud and underline each V/CV pattern.

IN SUMMARY You may want students to summarize the lesson in their own words. Elicit from students that a two-syllable word with the V/CV pattern usually has a long vowel sound in the first syllable; students can use this knowledge to predict how to write an unfamiliar word.

ASSIGNMENT Students can complete the first page of the lesson as a follow-up to the group activity, either in class or as homework.

Lesson 15: Patterns—V/CV Words *(continued)*

Practicing the Lesson

Spelling Clues: Proofreading Syllables

Suggest that when students proofread their spelling, they first say the entire word aloud and then pronounce its individual syllables. They should circle syllables that don't seem to match their pronunciation and then use a dictionary if necessary to check the spelling of the word.

Remind students that words having the V/CV pattern often have a long vowel sound in the first syllable, while words having the VC/CV pattern often have a short vowel sound in the first syllable. Write these word pairs on the board: *diner/dinner*; *super/supper*; and *later/latter*. Have students pronounce each word aloud and tell whether the initial syllable in the word has a long or a short vowel sound. Then have them identify the V/CV or VC/CV pattern in the word.

You may want to point out that the long *e* sound in *cheetah* and in *eager* is made with two vowel letters (*ee* and *ea*) and that the *pr* in *apron* is a cluster that functions as a single consonant. APPLYING SPELLING STRATEGIES

TRANSITIONAL SPELLERS Have students complete this activity with a partner, spelling their words aloud to each other as they review their answers.

Proofreading

You may wish to have students review Spelling Clues: Proofreading Syllables before proofreading the paragraph.

Fun with Words

Students may complete this activity individually or with a partner. Tell students not to use the Spelling Words they have written on lines 1–12.

Posttest

Administer the test on page 32 as a posttest, or administer one of your own. Say each word, use it in a sentence, and then repeat the word.

Reteaching the Lesson

Divide the Spelling Words into lists, one for each vowel sound heard at the beginning of the word. Have students read all the words in each list of Spelling Words. Tell them to stress the first syllable in each word as they say it, and then have them identify the vowel sound as long or short. After students have spelled the word aloud, have them say it one more time, underlining with their fingers the V/CV pattern as they pronounce the two syllables. AUDITORY MODALITY

(Pretest/Posttest, continued)

13. Shannon and her **rival** shook hands before the competition.

14. Upon what **basis** did you make your decision?

15. A **cheetah** is a member of the cat family.

16. The train trip offers a **scenic** view of the area.

PRACTICE ACTIVITY

The practice activity is on page 127.

Answers: Spelling Clues

1. eager **3.** Friday
2. basis **4.** rival

Answers: Proofreading

5. agent **9.** vital
6. scenic **10.** razor
7. meter **11.** local
8. cheetah **12.** evil

Answers: Fun with Words

13. apron **15.** fiber
14. motive **16.** famous

TEACHING STRATEGIES

Lesson 16: Adding *-ed* and *-ing*

OBJECTIVE

To spell words ending with *-ed* or *-ing*

HOME ACTIVITY

The home activity is on page 129.

SECOND-LANGUAGE SUPPORT

Forming the past tense of regular verbs by adding *-ed* can be difficult for students with limited English proficiency. It is important for students to recognize that *-ed* may be pronounced /t/ as in *looked* or /d/ as in *cleaned*. Have students brainstorm words with *-ed* and write them on the board. Then have students read each word aloud and say the ending clearly, underlining the *-ed* ending in each word as they pronounce it. COMPARING AND CONTRASTING

PRETEST/POSTTEST

1. I **lifted** the cover from the pot.
2. The soup is **cooling** now.
3. Sarah's **pointed** remark about hand-me-downs made me feel uncomfortable.
4. We **returned** the chairs we had borrowed for the party.
5. My brother is **speaking** on the telephone to his best friend.
6. Our class has a **spelling** test each week.
7. Mike **wondered** when the rain would stop.
8. Tina **bragged** about her good report card.
9. The cut on my finger **healed** quickly.
10. I **scrubbed** my hands with soap and water.
11. No one correctly **answered** every question on the test.
12. The rain **threatened** to spoil our plans.
13. We **admitted** that we were wrong.

(continued on next page)

Pretest

Administer the test on this page as a pretest. Say each word, use it in the sentence, and then repeat the word. ACCESSING PRIOR KNOWLEDGE

SELF-CHECK Have students check their own pretests against the list of Spelling Words. Remind students to write misspelled words in their Lesson Word Logs. STUDENT SELF-ASSESSMENT

Introducing the Lesson

Option A (Open Sort)

Distribute the word cards (page 128) to individuals or small groups, and guide them in an open-sort activity. In open sort, students group the word cards according to a criterion they select themselves. Then guide students in comparing and discussing the criteria they selected.

Option B (Modeling)

Read aloud with students the lesson title and the Spelling Words. Use this model sentence to introduce the lesson skill in a context.

*The car **stopped running** when it ran out of gas.*

Teaching the Lesson

- Ask volunteers to name some Spelling Words that end with *-ed* in which the base word does not change, as in *played*. List the words on the board. Then have volunteers name words that end with *-ing* in which the base word does not change. List those words on the board as well. *(**-ed:** lifted, pointed, returned, wondered, healed, answered, threatened; **-ing:** cooling, speaking, spelling)*
- Follow the same procedure with *-ed* and *-ing* words in which the final consonant is doubled before the ending is added. *(**-ed:** bragged, scrubbed, admitted, committed, preferred; **-ing:** referring)*
- After students add words from their own writing to the columns, have volunteers read the words, underline the *-ed* or *-ing* ending, and circle any doubled consonants.

IN SUMMARY You may want students to summarize the lesson in their own words. Elicit from students that if a word ends in a vowel and a consonant and the last syllable is accented, the final consonant is doubled before *-ed* or *-ing* is added.

ASSIGNMENT Students can complete the first page of the lesson as a follow-up activity, either in class or as homework.

Lesson 16: Adding *-ed* and *-ing* *(continued)*

Practicing the Lesson

Spelling Clues: Spelling Rules

Suggest to students that they recite the *-ed*/*-ing* rules to themselves or to a classmate before they begin the activity.

Remind students that when a word ends with vowel-consonant and the accent is on the final syllable, the consonant is usually doubled before *-ed* or *-ing* is added. In checking the second activity, therefore, students should first determine what the base word is and then apply the spelling rules. For example, in the case of the incorrect spelling *commited*, the base word is *commit*, which ends in vowel-consonant and has its second syllable accented. Therefore, the consonant before *-ed* must be doubled *(committed)*. APPLYING SPELLING STRATEGIES

TRANSITIONAL SPELLERS Have students complete this activity with a partner, explaining the rationale behind each spelling they decide on.

Proofreading

You may wish to have students review Spelling Clues: Spelling Rules before proofreading the notice.

Working with Meaning

Caution students not to use Spelling Words already used in lines 1–10. Suggest to students that they use sentence context to decide whether the Spelling Word to use requires an *-ed* or an *-ing* ending. The Spelling Dictionary can be used to check definitions.

SECOND-LANGUAGE SUPPORT Have students read the dialogue aloud with a partner. Then let them paraphrase the dialogue in their own words. PARAPHRASING

Posttest

Administer the test on page 34 as a posttest, or administer one of your own. Say each word, use it in a sentence, and then repeat the word.

Reteaching the Lesson

Divide the Spelling Words into lists, one for each different spelling. First, have students look at each word and say the word aloud. Then, have them look at the individual letters and say them aloud, stressing the final letters that spell the word's ending. Tell students to close their eyes and spell the word from memory. Finally, have them open their eyes and say and spell the word one more time. VISUAL MODALITY

(Pretest/Posttest, continued)

14. You'll get the job done if you are **committed** to it.

15. To which book are you **referring?**

16. Jill **preferred** swimming to jogging.

PRACTICE ACTIVITY

The practice activity is on page 130.

Answers: Spelling Clues

1. threatened **4.** cooling
2. lifted **5.** referring
3. scrubbed **6.** admitted

Answers: Proofreading

7. healed **9.** pointed
8. committed **10.** preferred

Answers: Working with Meaning

11. speaking **14.** wondered
12. spelling **15.** returned
13. answered **16.** bragged

Unit 3 Review

OBJECTIVES

- To review spelling patterns and strategies in Lessons 12–16
- To give students the opportunity to recognize and use these spelling patterns and Spelling Words in their writing

UNIT 3 WORDS

The following words are reviewed in Practice Test, Parts A and B.

Lesson 12: Changing *y* to *i*

supplies	occupied
families	denied

Lesson 13: Endings /ər/, /əl/, /ən/

Indian	musical
speaker	original

Lesson 14: Patterns—VC/CV Words

engine	further
pillow	convince

Lesson 15: Patterns—V/CV Words

apron	Friday
scenic	famous

Lesson 16: Adding *-ed* and *-ing*

threatened	preferred
committed	cooling

Review Strategies

Review with students the following spelling-clue strategies for Lessons 12–16.

Lesson 12 Spelling Clues: Spelling Rules

Write the word *supply* on the board. Ask volunteers to go to the board and write the words *supplies* and *supplied.* Then have them explain the rule they followed for adding the endings *-es* and *-ed.* Remind students that if a word ends in a consonant and *y,* the *y* is changed to *i* before *-es* or *-ed* is added.

Lesson 13 Spelling Clues: Best-Guess Spelling

Say the word *stretcher* aloud. Ask students to write their best guess for how the word is spelled. Let students with different answers write them on the board. Then have the class vote on the best guess. Remind students that when they spell an unfamiliar word, they can use their best guess and then check it in a dictionary.

Lesson 14 Spelling Clues: Syllabication

Write the word *monster* on the board. Have a volunteer divide the word into syllables (*mon/ster*). Emphasize that words having the VC/CV pattern are divided between the middle consonants but not between the letters of a consonant cluster or digraph.

Lesson 15 Spelling Clues: Proofreading Syllables

Write the word *famous* on the board. Compare spellings that may be different (*faymous* and *famous* for example), and have students choose the correct spelling. Remind them that breaking a word into syllables and checking the word one syllable at a time is helpful in spelling an unfamiliar word.

Lesson 16 Spelling Clues: Spelling Rules

Write the words *point* and *refer* on the board. Have volunteers write the words *pointed* and *referring* on the board. Ask them what rules they followed for spelling the endings. (The *-ed* ending can be added to *point* without any changes. The final *r* in *refer* is doubled because *refer* ends in a vowel and a consonant and the accent is on the second syllable.) Stress the importance of applying spelling rules when adding endings to words.

Unit 3 Review *(continued)*

Practice Test

The Practice Test provides an opportunity to review Spelling Words and spelling generalizations in a standardized test format, complete with a sample answer card.

Option 1

Use Practice Test: Part A as a pretest. Later, use Practice Test: Part B as a posttest.

Option 2

Have students review their Lesson Word Log for this unit. If they need extra help, you may wish to review the spelling generalizations discussed in the individual lessons. Then administer both parts of the Practice Test to determine whether students have mastered the spelling generalizations.

Practice Test: Part A

1. (B) apron
2. (A) supplies
3. (D) families
4. (C) occupied
5. (A) threatened
6. (B) Indian
7. (D) speaker
8. (C) musical
9. (D) engine
10. (C) pillow

Practice Test: Part B

1. (D) further
2. (C) scenic
3. (B) convince
4. (C) committed
5. (A) Friday
6. (A) original
7. (D) denied
8. (B) preferred
9. (C) famous
10. (C) cooling

Options for Evaluation

- Have students check their own Practice Tests against their lists of Spelling Words. The list on the opposite page provides references to the lessons where they can find words they misspelled.
- You may prefer to assign partners and have students check each other's Practice Tests, using their own list of Spelling Words.

REVIEW ACTIVITIES

Activity 1

Organize students in small groups to play a version of "Twenty Questions" that uses the words from this review lesson. One member of the group chooses a word, and other group members then try to guess it. Students may ask only "yes" and "no" questions. For example: "Does the word have two syllables?" "Does the word begin with a vowel?" "Does the word have a double consonant in it?" The student who finally guesses the word should read it aloud and then choose another word for group members to guess.

Activity 2

Invite a student to choose a word from this review lesson and then say aloud within one minute as many words as possible that rhyme with the word. Other students should listen to the list of words and then guess the word. After the word has been guessed, students should spell the word aloud.

Activity 3

Have students who need a reteaching activity write on individual index cards each word from this review lesson. Then tell students to sort the cards according to the spelling generalizations that are presented in each lesson in Unit 3. Later, invite students to display their categorized cards and explain how they sorted the words for each lesson.

Activity 4

Let students play a game of "Charades" in small groups, using the words from this review lesson. Each student chooses a word to act out. Gestures may be based on the word's meaning or on its spelling. A student who guesses the word and spells it correctly can be the one to lead the next round of "Charades."

Unit 3 Review *(continued)*

WHAT'S IN A WORD?

castle

Have students work in small groups to create "castle" stories. Later, invite students to tell what two or more of the stories have in common in terms of plot, character, or theme.

♦ escape

Have students work in small groups to compile lists of movies, books, and plays where a character is trying to escape from something or someone.

meditation

You may wish to provide students with a thesaurus to discover more synonyms for *meditation.* Encourage students to use each synonym in a sentence.

♦ This indicates a Unit Spelling Word.

Unit Activity Options

Partner Spelling

If a student writes the wrong answer for a partner's clue, have the first student explain his or her reasoning. Then let the partner rewrite the clue to make it clearer.

Spelling Cards

Encourage students to explain how they decided on the spelling they chose for each word.

Say It Quickly

Review the game rules with students. Guide them in agreeing on the specific number prefixes and combining forms to use in the game. You may also want to have volunteers suggest a few words that begin with each number prefix or combining form and that are not covered in this lesson. Then have students form groups of five or six and play the game.

Pick a Card, Any Card

You may want to add more words with *-ed* and *-ing* endings to the deck of cards.

WORKING TOGETHER You may want to pair students of different levels of spelling proficiency for the Pick a Card, Any Card activity.

A Final Scramble

You may want to extend the activity by selecting one scrambled form of each Spelling Word and giving copies of the list to all students for unscrambling.

Proofreading Partners

Encourage partners to discuss their ideas for paragraphs. Remind them that, to include the listed words, they may need to create an unusual or even a fantastic situation in their paragraphs.

OPTIONS

Unit 3 Review *(continued)*

Curriculum Options

Language Arts: Headline Search

Organize students into small groups. Give each group one or more newspapers. Challenge them to look at the headline above each article and try to find consonant *-y* words in which the *-es* or *-ed* ending has been added. (Example: Mayor Studies New Tax Plan) Tell each group to list the words it discovers. Later, have group members display their headlines and read them aloud, challenging classmates to find the word in each headline that follows the spelling rule from the lesson. If you wish, make the activity a contest in which the group that identifies the most words wins.

Science: Word Experiments

Organize students into small or large groups. Have each group find a science experiment described either in their science textbook or in another science resource. Tell students to go through the steps of the experiment and list words with the V/CV pattern that appear in the text. Later, invite each group to write its V/CV words on the board. Then, invite group members to explain the experiment to classmates in their own words, using the V/CV words from their list in their explanation. If possible, let each group not only describe its experiment but perform it for classmates as well.

Social Studies: Reporter's Investigation

Organize students into small groups. Tell group members to imagine they are investigative reporters searching for information. Have them choose an article from a social studies textbook or from a newspaper or magazine. (All groups may choose the same article.) Students should look for and list any VC/CV words that appear in their article. Later, invite each group to list its VC/CV words on the board. If all groups used the same article, see which group found the most words. If groups used different articles, invite students to summarize their article for classmates, using as many of the VC/CV words from their list as possible in their summary.

WHAT'S IN A WORD?

mesmerize

Have students brainstorm in small groups to list stories in which sleep or dreams are an important part of the plot. Encourage students to briefly summarize the plot of each story.

museum

Suggest that students use the computer or card catalog in their school library to name stories, books, or plays involving a museum. Or, as an alternative to listing fiction stories, they may list nonfiction books about museums.

phobia

Encourage students to brainstorm a list of stories with a partner or in a small group. Since most stories involve a problem that a character must solve, supplying an adequate list of story titles should not be difficult for students. Encourage them to describe briefly the plot of each story to classmates.

Lesson 18: Noun Suffix *-ance/-ence*

OBJECTIVE

To spell words with the suffix *-ance* or *-ence*

HOME ACTIVITY

The home activity is on page 132.

SECOND-LANGUAGE SUPPORT

Remind students that in English the same sound can almost always be spelled in more than one way. List the following pairs of words on the board: inst*ant*, inst*ance*; differ*ent*, differ*ence*; abs*ent*, abs*ence*.

Tell students that while there is no rule governing whether to use *-ance* or *-ence*, the spelling consistently matches that of the related adjective forms, for example, inst*ant*/inst*ance*. RECOGNIZING SPELLING PATTERNS

PRETEST/POSTTEST

1. Please explain the **importance** of careful spelling.
2. The singer made her **entrance** to the sound of applause.
3. What's the **difference** between a colt and a pony?
4. India wanted **independence** from England.
5. Mom's company provides health **insurance** for the whole family.
6. The English teachers are attending a reading **conference.**
7. An **ambulance** raced to the scene of the accident.
8. You have one **absence** so far this semester.
9. In one **instance,** the boys rescued a cat from a tree.
10. The **audience** applauded after the chorus sang.
11. Do you have to do chores to earn your **allowance**?
12. Is good spelling a mark of **intelligence**?

(continued on next page)

Pretest

Administer the test on this page as a pretest. Say each word, use it in the sentence, and then repeat the word. ACCESSING PRIOR KNOWLEDGE

SELF-CHECK Have students check their own pretests against the list of Spelling Words. Remind students to write misspelled words in their Lesson Word Logs. STUDENT SELF-ASSESSMENT

Introducing the Lesson

Option A (Open Sort)

Distribute the word cards (page 131) to individuals or small groups, and guide them in an open-sort activity. In open sort, students group the word cards according to a criterion they select themselves. Then, guide students in comparing and discussing the criteria they selected.

Option B (Modeling)

Read aloud with students the lesson title and the Spelling Words. Use this model sentence to introduce the lesson skill in a context.

*Her **reluctance** to continue the **correspondence** was a disappointment.*

Teaching the Lesson

- Have students name some Spelling Words that have the same suffix as the word *fragrance*. As students name words, list them on the board under the heading *fragrance*. *(importance, entrance, insurance, ambulance, instance, allowance, assurance, appearance)*
- Follow the same procedure for words that have the same suffix as the word *excellence*. *(difference, independence, conference, absence, audience, intelligence, obedience, presence)*
- After students add words from their own reading or writing to the columns, have volunteers read aloud all the words and underline the endings.

IN SUMMARY You may want students to summarize the lesson in their own words. Elicit from students that the suffix *-ance* or *-ence* is a noun ending meaning "quality of" or "state of." Since there are no rules governing which spelling to use, a dictionary is necessary to check for accuracy.

ASSIGNMENT Students can complete the first page of the lesson as a follow-up to the group activity, either in class or as homework.

Lesson 18: Noun Suffix *-ance/-ence* (continued)

Practicing the Lesson

Spelling Clues: Words with Suffixes

Point out to students that when it comes to spelling words that end in *-ance* or *-ence,* memorization and the use of a dictionary are probably the best methods they can use.

Another strategy they might try is to pronounce the word in their minds, exaggerating the vowel of the ending to emphasize its spelling. Suggest that they try this as they study the Spelling Words this week.

Have students pair off and practice this approach. A student reads one Spelling Word at a time to the partner, stressing short *a* or short *e* as appropriate. After the student has read a word aloud, the partner spells the word. Then the students reverse roles and go on to the next word in the list. APPLYING SPELLING STRATEGIES

TRANSITIONAL SPELLERS Have students divide the words into two columns: *-ance* endings and *-ence* endings. Then have them write each word three times, saying the word in their minds each time as they spell it.

Proofreading

You may wish to have students review Spelling Clues: Words with Suffixes before proofreading the advertisement.

Fun with Words

Have students complete the cartoon with Spelling Words they have not already written on lines 1–12. You may want to have students create their own cartoons, using Spelling Words or other words that follow the generalization.

Posttest

Administer the test on page 40 as a posttest, or administer one of your own. Say each word, use it in a sentence, and then repeat the word.

Reteaching the Lesson

Write these words on the board: *absent, appear, confer, import, intelligent, allow, assure, differ, instant, obedient, independent.* Have students change the words into a form that means "the quality of" or "the state of." For example, they can change *absent* to *absence.* Have them write the ending with a colored pencil or marker. When students have written each Spelling Word, have them exchange papers and check one another's work. VISUAL MODALITY

(Pretest/Posttest, continued)

13. She gave her **assurance** that she would be there on time.
14. Wally had the right **appearance** for the part.
15. I took my frisky dog to school to learn **obedience.**
16. We felt the poet's **presence** even before he arrived.

PRACTICE ACTIVITY

The practice activity is on page 133.

Answers: Spelling Clues

1. presence
2. insurance
3. conference
4. assurance
5. allowance
6. importance

Answers: Proofreading

7. independence
8. intelligence
9. difference
10. obedience
11. instance
12. absence

Answers: Fun with Words

13. entrance
14. appearance
15. ambulance
16. audience

Lesson 19: Noun Suffixes *-ship, -ment, -ity*

OBJECTIVE

To spell words with the suffixes *-ship, -ment,* and *-ity*

HOME ACTIVITY

The home activity is on page 135.

SECOND-LANGUAGE SUPPORT

Some students find it hard to hear the difference between a final *t* (as in *argument*) and a final *d* (as in *depend*). Others find it hard to distinguish between a final *t* (as in *commit*) and a final *p* (as in *leadership*). Write these groups of words on the board and pronounce them with students: *cot/cod/cop; hit/hid/hip; sat/sad/sap;* and *beet/bead/beep.* Then have students identify Spelling Words that have a final *t* or a final *p* sound. COMPARING AND CONTRASTING

PRETEST/POSTTEST

1. The senator made a short **statement** to the press.
2. We celebrate **friendship** as well as love on Valentine's Day.
3. Ms. Allen attended a forum on **leadership** at the college.
4. Students worked in **partnership** with teachers to choose books for the library.
5. My parents let me pursue only one after-school **activity.**
6. Some people are gifted with natural artistic **ability.**
7. The manager and umpire are having a friendly **argument.**
8. Her **personality** won her many friends.
9. The storm knocked out the **electricity.**
10. She won the local **championship** in figure-skating.
11. All kinds of people make up our **community.**
12. I voted with the **majority.**

(continued on next page)

Pretest

Administer the test on this page as a pretest. Say each word, use it in the sentence, and then repeat the word. ACCESSING PRIOR KNOWLEDGE

SELF-CHECK Have students check their own pretests against the list of Spelling Words. Remind students to write misspelled words in their Lesson Word Logs. STUDENT SELF-ASSESSMENT

Introducing the Lesson

Option A (Open Sort)

Distribute the word cards (page 134) to individuals or small groups, and guide them in an open-sort activity. In open sort, students group the word cards according to a criterion they select themselves. Then, guide students in comparing and discussing the criteria they selected.

Option B (Modeling)

Read aloud with students the lesson title and the Spelling Words. Use this model sentence to introduce the lesson skill in a context.

*The **quality** of the chess player was evident at the **tournament**.*

Teaching the Lesson

- Ask volunteers to name some Spelling Words that have the same suffix as the word *fellowship*. As students name words, list them on the board under the heading *fellowship*. *(friendship, leadership, partnership, championship)*
- Follow the same procedure for the words *movement* and *felicity*. *(**movement:** statement, argument; **felicity:** activity, ability, personality, electricity, community, majority, responsibility, curiosity, necessity, authority)*
- After students add words from their own reading or writing to the columns, have volunteers read aloud all the words and underline the suffixes.

IN SUMMARY Encourage students to summarize the lesson in their own words. Elicit from students that most words retain their spelling when the suffix *-ship* or *-ment* is added. However, the spelling of the base word usually changes if it ends in *e* and the suffix *-ity* is added.

ASSIGNMENT Students can complete the first page of the lesson as a follow-up to the group activity, either in class or as homework.

Lesson 19: Noun Suffixes *-ship, -ment, -ity* *(continued)*

Practicing the Lesson

Spelling Clues: Suffixes

Remind students that the spelling of a base word may change when a suffix is added, or it may not. Then teach them the following generalization: When a suffix *beginning* with a vowel is added to a base word *ending* with a vowel, the base word usually changes. Share these examples with students: *active* + *-ity* = *activity, commune* + *-ity* = *community, able* + *-ity* = *ability, responsible* + *-ity* = *responsibility, curious* + *-ity* = *curiosity.*

Then follow the same process using the suffix *-ment* (which begins with a consonant). Use the base words *state* and *move.* (You may want to point out that the word *argument* is an exception to the general rule. The *e* in *argue* is dropped before the suffix *-ment* is added.) APPLYING SPELLING STRATEGIES

Proofreading

You may wish to have students review Spelling Clues: Suffixes before proofreading the notice.

Working with Meaning

After students have completed the activity, you may want to have them rewrite part or all of the paragraph using three or four other words that end in *-ship*, *-ment*, or *-ity*. For example, students might write, *Mrs. Lee and I have had a* friendship *for many years. I admire her* ability *to avoid an* argument.

Posttest

Administer the test on page 42 as a posttest, or administer one of your own. Say each word, use it in a sentence, and then repeat the word.

Reteaching the Lesson

Write the suffixes *-ship, -ment,* and *-ity* and the base words for the Spelling Words on separate 3 × 5 cards. Place the cards in two boxes, one labeled *Base Word* and the other labeled *Suffix.* Begin by putting the suffixes *-ment* and *-ship* in the box along with base words that will not require a change. Later, add the suffix *-ity,* which begins with a vowel, and the base word for the word that is an exception to the rule *(argument).*

Have the student select at random a card from each box, put the two pieces together, and read the word. If the word does not exist, have the student return one card to the box and choose another. When the student forms a real word, have the student say the word, spell it aloud, and write it. KINESTHETIC MODALITY

(Pretest/Posttest, continued)

13. It's not Brad's **responsibility** to take out the trash.

14. The cat's **curiosity** led it into trouble.

15. Umbrellas are a **necessity** in Wisconsin, but not in Arizona.

16. Mr. Jackson has the **authority** to cancel the dance.

PRACTICE ACTIVITY

The practice activity is on page 136.

Answers: Spelling Clues

1. statement	**4.** partnership
2. authority	**5.** electricity
3. majority	**6.** argument

Answers: Proofreading

7. championship	**10.** ability
8. friendship	**11.** activity
9. curiosity	**12.** necessity

Answers: Working with Meaning

13. community	**15.** responsibility
14. leadership	**16.** personality

Lesson 20: Prefix *ad- (ac-, as-, af-, ap-)*

OBJECTIVE

To spell words with the prefix *ad- (ac-, as-, af-, ap-)*

HOME ACTIVITY

The home activity is on page 138.

SECOND-LANGUAGE SUPPORT

In Spanish, consonants are not doubled unless, like *ll* and *rr*, they represent a different sound than the single consonant or unless both consonants are sounded. The Spanish equivalent of *assistance*, for example, is *asistencia*, whereas the Spanish equivalent of *accident* is *accidente*, because both c's are sounded.) Therefore, students whose native language is Spanish may need extra practice with this particular kind of sound/letter correspondence in English. SOUND-LETTER CORRESPONDENCES

PRETEST/POSTTEST

1. Mrs. Rose **appointed** Mr. Ward as acting principal during her absence.
2. Lou broke his hand in a backstage **accident.**
3. The home economics class prepared dessert for the gala **affair.**
4. We're having a school **assembly** tomorrow.
5. Don't **approach** an injured animal.
6. Did he **accuse** you of lying?
7. At the end of Act I, there was loud **applause.**
8. The baby shows great **affection** for her grandmother.
9. I will **accompany** you to the office.
10. Your teacher may **assign** a book report.
11. Most people **appreciate** acts of kindness.
12. Check that your spelling is **accurate.**

(continued on next page)

Pretest

Administer the test on this page as a pretest. Say each word, use it in the sentence, and then repeat the word. ACCESSING PRIOR KNOWLEDGE

SELF-CHECK Have students check their own pretests against the list of Spelling Words. Remind students to write misspelled words in their Lesson Word Logs. STUDENT SELF-ASSESSMENT

Introducing the Lesson

Option A (Open Sort)

Distribute the word cards (page 137) to individuals or small groups, and guide them in an open-sort activity. In open sort, students group the word cards according to a criterion they select themselves. Then, guide students in comparing and discussing the criteria they selected.

Option B (Modeling)

Read aloud with students the lesson title and the Spelling Words. Use this model sentence to introduce the lesson skill in a context.

*The officer **affirmed** that the thief had been **apprehended.***

Teaching the Lesson

- Tell students that the prefix *ad-* comes from Latin and means "to." When it is joined to an English word, it can be spelled *ac-*, *as-*, *af-*, or *ap-*, depending upon what letter the root word begins with.
- Ask volunteers to name Spelling Words in which the prefix is spelled the way it is in ac*cept*. List the words on the board. *(accident, accuse, accompany, accurate, accustomed)*
- Follow the same procedure for the Spelling Words that begin with *as-*, *af-*, and *ap-*. *(**as-:** assembly, assign, association, assistance; **af-:** affair, affection; **ap-:** appointed, approach, applause, appreciate, apparent)*
- After students have added words from their own reading or writing to the columns, call on volunteers to underline the prefixes. SORTING WORDS

IN SUMMARY Encourage students to summarize the lesson in their own words. Elicit from students that the prefix *ad-* may be spelled *ac-*, *as-*, *af-*, or *ap-* and that the spelling of the prefix depends on the consonant that begins the root.

ASSIGNMENT Students can complete the first page of the lesson as a follow-up activity, either in class or as homework.

Lesson 20: Prefix *ad- (ac-, as-, af-, ap-)* (continued)

Practicing the Lesson

Spelling Clues: Words with Prefixes

Tell students that these prefixes are absorbed prefixes; they don't stand out because the roots and prefixes have been linked for so long. Remind students that each Spelling Word has a double consonant where the prefix joins the root. Tell students to begin their proofreading task by checking for the double consonant. Then have them break each word into parts and check each part to see that it is spelled correctly.

Work through an example or two with students. The following Spelling Words exemplify the process well: *as + sist + ance, ap + point + ed.* APPLYING SPELLING STRATEGIES

Proofreading

You may wish to have students review Spelling Clues: Words with Prefixes before proofreading the letter.

Fun with Words

Have students complete the activity individually or with a partner. Be sure students understand that the underlined word is a synonym or near-synonym for the root of the word that is the correct response. (For example, *guests* is a synonym for *company*, the root of *accompany*.)

Posttest

Administer the test on page 44 as a posttest, or administer one of your own. Say each word, use it in a sentence, and then repeat the word.

Reteaching the Lesson

Write the Spelling Words on the board. Then, ask volunteers to separate the words into syllables using slash marks. (Make sure they divide words between the double consonants.) Next, read the words, one syllable at a time, to students as they spell the word on paper without looking at the board. After each word, have students look up and check their work and circle those words they misspelled. When students have spelled all the words, have them copy those they missed, one syllable at a time, from the board. After they have studied the words, repeat the exercise. KINESTHETIC MODALITY

(Pretest/Posttest, continued)

13. The PTA is an **association** of parents and teachers.
14. It became **apparent** that Betsy hadn't studied for the test.
15. People here are not **accustomed** to this much rain.
16. Please lend your **assistance** when it is needed.

PRACTICE ACTIVITY

The practice activity is on page 139.

Answers: Spelling Clues

1. accident
2. applause
3. approach
4. association
5. assembly
6. accustomed
7. assistance
8. appreciate

Answers: Proofreading

9. appointed
10. accuse
11. accurate
12. affection

Answers: Fun with Words

13. affair
14. accompany
15. assign
16. apparent

Lesson 21: Prefix *com- (con-)*

OBJECTIVE

To spell words that begin with the prefix *com- (con-)*

HOME ACTIVITY

The home activity is on page 141.

SECOND-LANGUAGE SUPPORT

Students may have trouble distinguishing between the sounds of *m* and *n* in the medial position. The problem is exaggerated when the consonant is not clearly pronounced, as may happen when words such as *confusing* or *conviction* are said rapidly. Write the Spelling Words, one at a time, on the board. Read each word for students, clearly voicing the *m* or *n*. Underline the *m* or *n*. Then have students repeat the word and spell it aloud, emphasizing the *m* or *n*. MAKING SOUND-LETTER CONNECTIONS

PRETEST/POSTTEST

1. Martin spoke with **conviction** when he talked of civil rights.
2. The general **commanded** the army to retreat.
3. They **commonly** run around the track at lunchtime.
4. We **considered** going skating but instead settled on swimming.
5. The rain **continued** all day.
6. The **commander** earned the respect of his troops.
7. I cannot **commit** myself to being there.
8. Our school **constitution** was written by the first class to graduate.
9. The instruction booklet is very **confusing.**
10. The party will **commence** when all the guests arrive.
11. The monkeys created so much **commotion** that we could barely hear the zookeeper.

(continued on next page)

Pretest

Administer the test on this page as a pretest. Say each word, use it in the sentence, and then repeat the word. ACCESSING PRIOR KNOWLEDGE

SELF-CHECK Have students check their own pretests against the list of Spelling Words. Remind students to write misspelled words in their Lesson Word Logs. STUDENT SELF-ASSESSMENT

Introducing the Lesson

Option A (Open Sort)

Distribute the word cards (page 140) to individuals or small groups, and guide them in an open-sort activity. In open sort, students group the word cards according to a criterion they select themselves. Then, guide students in comparing and discussing the criteria they selected.

Option B (Modeling)

Read aloud with students the lesson title and the Spelling Words. Use this model sentence to introduce the lesson skill in a context.

__Commerce__ between the two cities will __continue.__

Teaching the Lesson

- Tell students that the prefix *com-* or *con-* means "together" or "with."
- Ask volunteers to name Spelling Words that have the same prefix as the word *commune. (commanded, commonly, commander, commit, commence, commotion, commercial, communicate, communities, communication, committee)*
- Follow the same procedure for Spelling Words that have the same prefix as the word *constant. (conviction, considered, continued, constitution, confusing)*
- After students have added words from their own reading or writing to the columns, call on volunteers to read all the words aloud and underline the prefixes.

IN SUMMARY Encourage students to summarize the lesson in their own words. Elicit from students that the prefix *com-* or *con-* means "together" or "with" and that words that begin with *com* have a double *m* if the prefix is joined to a root that begins with *m*.

ASSIGNMENT Students can complete the first page of the lesson as a follow-up to the group activity, either in class or as homework.

Lesson 21: Prefix *com-* (*con-*) *(continued)*

Practicing the Lesson

Spelling Clues: Prefixes

Tell students to read the Spelling Words and listen for the consonants that link the prefix to the root in each word. Ask them how they can tell if there is a double consonant. (They hear only one consonant sound, not two different sounds, where the prefix attaches to the root.) When *con-* is added to a root that begins with *n*, the word is usually spelled with a double *n*.

Have students add the correct form of the prefix meaning "with" or "together" to each word part. Because *com-* (*con-*) is an absorbed prefix, students may have trouble recognizing it as a prefix, but they may be able to recognize the concept of togetherness in words like *community, constitution, committee,* and *communication*. APPLYING SPELLING STRATEGIES

Proofreading

You may wish to have students review Spelling Clues: Prefixes before proofreading the dialogue.

Working with Meaning

Have students complete the activity with words they have not yet written on lines 1–11. Encourage students to write paragraphs of their own, leaving blanks for at least four Spelling Words. Have them trade papers with a classmate and have the other student fill in the missing words.

Posttest

Administer the test on page 46 as a posttest, or administer one of your own. Say each word, use it in a sentence, and then repeat the word.

Reteaching the Lesson

Prepare a stack of cards on which you have written either *com-* or *con-*. Place the stack near the board along with some adhesive tape. Then, write the Spelling Words on the board, leaving off the first three letters of each word. Mix those beginning with *m* with those beginning with *n*. Call on volunteers to read a word part, choose the correct form of the prefix, and tape it before the word part.

For example, if *munication* is the word part, a student selects *com-* and places it in front of the word part. Next, the student reads the word aloud, spells it, and repeats it. When students have completed all the words on the board, ask them to tell what is the same about all the words that took the prefix *com-*. (They all have roots that begin with *m*.) VISUAL/KINESTHETIC MODALITY

(Pretest/Posttest, continued)

12. They interrupted the program with a **commercial.**
13. Babies usually **communicate** their unhappiness.
14. Many **communities** provide activities for young people.
15. We surely aid **communication** when we speak honestly.
16. A **committee** was formed to clean up the school grounds.

PRACTICE ACTIVITY

The practice activity is on page 142.

Answers: Spelling Clues

1. constitution
2. commander
3. communities
4. commonly
5. commence
6. commercial

Answers: Proofreading

7. continued
8. commotion
9. committee
10. commit
11. considered

Answers: Working with Meaning

12. communication
13. commanded
14. communicate
15. confusing
16. conviction

Lesson 22: Unstressed Ending *-ant/-ent*

OBJECTIVE
To spell words that end in *-ant* or *-ent*

HOME ACTIVITY
The home activity is on page 144.

SECOND-LANGUAGE SUPPORT
Remind students that in English, the same sound can almost always be spelled in more than one way. Write the following chart on the board:

import*ance*	inst*ance*
differ*ence*	independ*ence*
abs*ence*	obedi*ence*

Tell students that while there is no rule governing whether to use *-ant* or *-ent*, the spelling of an adjective form consistently matches that of a related noun form. Have students spell the related adjective form of each noun above. RECOGNIZING SPELLING PATTERNS

PRETEST/POSTTEST
1. Three people were **absent** yesterday.
2. It is **important** to use cursive when you sign your name.
3. She likes to dress in the **current** style.
4. We elected our class **president** last Monday.
5. The **elephant** trumpeted its displeasure.
6. Laurel feels **confident** that she will make the team.
7. I brought some **instant** lemonade.
8. It has been a long time since scientists discovered a new **element.**
9. Mr. O'Day did not treat Big Sam like a **servant.**
10. Tommy Lee got an **excellent** grade on the math test.
11. Did the tennis player beat her **opponent**?

(continued on next page)

Pretest
Administer the test on this page as a pretest. Say each word, use it in the sentence, and then repeat the word. ACCESSING PRIOR KNOWLEDGE

SELF-CHECK Have students check their own pretests against the list of Spelling Words. Remind students to write misspelled words in their Lesson Word Logs. STUDENT SELF-ASSESSMENT

Introducing the Lesson
Option A (Open Sort)
Distribute the word cards (page 143) to individuals or small groups and guide them in an open-sort activity. In open sort, students group the word cards according to a criterion they select themselves. Then, guide students in comparing and discussing the criteria they selected.

Option B (Modeling)
Read aloud with students the lesson title and the Spelling Words. Use this model sentence to introduce the lesson skill in a context.

*The **relevant** details are in this **independent** study.*

Teaching the Lesson
- Ask volunteers to name some Spelling Words that end like the word *dominant*. As students name words, list them on the board under the heading *dominant. (important, elephant, instant, servant, assistant, significant)*
- Follow the same procedure for words that end like *different. (absent, current, president, confident, element, excellent, opponent, permanent, innocent, sufficient)*
- After students add words from their own reading or writing to the columns, have volunteers read aloud all the words and underline the spelling of each word's ending.

IN SUMMARY You may want students to summarize the lesson in their own words. Elicit from students that there is no rule to establish whether the ending *-ant* or *-ent* is correct, but knowing the correct spelling of a related word is helpful.

ASSIGNMENT Students can complete the first page of the lesson as a follow-up to the group activity, either in class or as homework.

Lesson 22: Unstressed Ending *-ant/-ent* *(continued)*

Practicing the Lesson

Spelling Clues: Mnemonics

Point out to students that when they have to spell words that end in *-ant* or *-ent*, memorization is one of the few methods they can use. Another is mnemonics.

Read the example on page 95 of the Pupil's Edition. Then help students as a group create one or two mnemonic devices before they do the activity individually. For example, students might come up with "I *can't* find anything signific*ant*" or "It's an excell*ent* t*ent*." APPLYING SPELLING STRATEGIES

TRANSITIONAL SPELLERS Have students write the words in two columns: *-ant* endings and *-ent* endings. Tell students to say the words with their eyes closed, one word at a time, not the way the words are actually pronounced, but with an emphatic short *e* or an emphatic short *a*. After visualizing each word, they should open their eyes and write it. Check their work for accuracy.

Proofreading

You may wish to have students review Spelling Clues: Mnemonics before proofreading the headlines.

Fun with Words

Have students complete the limerick with Spelling Words they have not already written on lines 1–12. You may want to have students create their own limericks, using Spelling Words or other words that follow the generalization.

Posttest

Administer the test on page 48 as a posttest, or administer one of your own. Say each word, use it in a sentence, and then repeat the word.

Reteaching the Lesson

Write the Spelling Words on the board, and have students write them in pencil on 3 × 5 cards, one word per card. Then have students go over each word with a marking pen, using a bright color for the *a* or *e* in the suffix and black or blue for all other letters in the words. On the reverse side of each card, have them write some related word, such as *currency* for *current* and *elephantine* for *elephant.* When they have written each Spelling Word, have them hand the stack to another student, who shows them the word on the reverse side of the card and asks them to spell the Spelling Word. VISUAL MODALITY

(Pretest/Posttest, continued)

12. These seating assignments are **permanent.**
13. Stephen hired an **assistant** to help him finish the work.
14. The kitten looked **innocent,** but the broken vase suggested guilt.
15. Dr. Sanchez made a **significant** discovery.
16. I don't have **sufficient** flour for this recipe.

PRACTICE ACTIVITY

The practice activity is on page 145.

Answers: Spelling Clues

1. elephant
2. absent
3. president
4. permanent
5. servant
6. opponent

Answers: Proofreading

7. current
8. significant
9. element
10. assistant
11. confident
12. instant

Answers: Fun with Words

13. confident
14. excellent
15. important
16. sufficient

Unit 4 Review

OBJECTIVES

- To review spelling patterns and strategies in Lessons 18–22
- To give students the opportunity to recognize and use these spelling patterns and Spelling Words in their writing

UNIT 4 WORDS

The following words are reviewed in Practice Test, Parts A and B.

Lesson 18: Noun Suffix *-ance/-ence*

intelligence, entrance, absence, presence

Lesson 19: Noun Suffixes *-ship, -ment, -ity*

necessity, statement, electricity, curiosity, leadership

Lesson 20: Prefix *ad- (ac-, as-, af-, ap-)*

applause, appreciate, assistance, assembly

Lesson 21: Prefix *com- (con-)*

communities, confusing, committee

Lesson 22: Unstressed Ending *-ant/-ent*

excellent, elephant, assistant, sufficient

Review Strategies

Review with students the following spelling-clue strategies for Lessons 18–22.

Lesson 18 Spelling Clues: Words with Suffixes

Say the word *conference* aloud. Invite several students to write the word on the board. Compare the spellings. If they are different *(conferance* and *conference,* for example), let the class decide which is correct. Suggest that if students are unsure whether a word ending is spelled *-ance* or *-ence,* they should consult a dictionary.

Lesson 19 Spelling Clues: Suffixes

Write the words *state* and *argue* on the board. Invite volunteers to add the suffix *-ment* to each word and to spell the words on the board. Have them tell which base word changed its spelling before the ending was added *(argue).* Remind students to check the spelling of the suffix and then decide whether the spelling of the base word changes when they write the new word.

Lesson 20 Spelling Clues: Words with Prefixes

Ask students to listen carefully as you say this sentence: *I appreciate the assistance and affection I got from the doctor after my accident.* Have students identify words that contain a prefix *(appreciate, assistance, affection, accident).* Have volunteers write the words on the board. What do they notice about the consonant in each prefix? (It is doubled.) Point out that a double consonant often occurs when a word begins with a variation of *ad-.*

Lesson 21 Spelling Clues: Prefixes

Ask students to listen carefully as you say this sentence: *The commander listened to the report from the committee.* Have students identify words that contain a prefix *(commander, committee).* Have volunteers write the words on the board. What do they notice about the consonant in each prefix? (It is doubled.) Point out that a double consonant often occurs when a word begins with *com-.*

Lesson 22 Spelling Clues: Mnemonics

Ask students what three-letter word they find in *elephant (ant).* Write this sentence on the board: An *elephant* is much larger than an *ant.* Point out that this observation can help them remember that the spelling is *elephant,* not *elephent.* Stress the idea that spelling tricks, or mnemonics, are a helpful way of remembering how to spell a word.

Unit 4 Review *(continued)*

Practice Test

The Practice Test provides an opportunity to review Spelling Words and spelling generalizations in a standardized test format, complete with a sample answer card.

Option 1

Use Practice Test: Part A as a pretest. Later, use Practice Test: Part B as a posttest.

Option 2

Have students review their Lesson Word Log for this unit. If they need extra help, you may wish to review the spelling generalizations discussed in the individual lessons. Then administer both parts of the Practice Test to determine whether students have mastered the spelling generalizations.

Practice Test: Part A

1. (B) intelligence
2. (C) necessity
3. (A) absence
4. (B) applause
5. (A) electricity
6. (A) assistance
7. (C) excellent
8. (D) communities
9. (D) leadership
10. (C) appreciate

Practice Test: Part B

1. (A) commitee [committee]
2. (B) confussing [confusing]
3. (A) statment [statement]
4. (A) asistant [assistant]
5. (B) elephent [elephant]
6. (A) sufficent [sufficient]
7. (B) entrence [entrance]
8. (B) curiocity [curiosity]
9. (A) assembily [assembly]
10. (A) presense [presence]

Options for Evaluation

- Have students check their own Practice Tests against their lists of Spelling Words. The list on the opposite page provides references to the lessons where they can find words they misspelled.
- You may prefer to assign partners and have students check each other's Practice Test, using their own list of Spelling Words.

REVIEW ACTIVITIES

Activity 1

Have students write each word from this review lesson on a separate index card. Shuffle all cards thoroughly, and pass them out to students, one card per person. Then tell students to display their cards to classmates and group themselves according to the spelling generalizations taught in the lessons. For example, the student holding the card that says *intelligence* and the student holding the card that says *absence* should stand together. After all students are in their proper groups, let each student read his or her card and spell the word aloud.

Activity 2

Have a volunteer choose a word from this review lesson and spell it aloud backward. Challenge other students to listen carefully to the letters to see if they can identify the word being spelled without writing the letters on paper. Suggest that students use the visualizing technique to help them picture the word's letters in their minds. The student who says the word and then spells it correctly can be the next player to spell another word backward.

Activity 3

Have students write the words from this review lesson on individual index cards. Then tell them to purposely misspell the same words on a second set of index cards. Mix all the cards together. Display a card and ask students whether the word is spelled correctly. If not, have them give the correct spelling.

Activity 4

Say the beginning of a word from this review lesson aloud, and let students say the rest of the word. For example, say *electri-* and have students say *city.* Then have a volunteer say the entire word and spell it aloud. A student may also choose a word to say partially and then let classmates say the entire word and spell it.

Unit 4 Review *(continued)*

WHAT'S IN A WORD?

♦ *ambulance*

Extend the activity by having students list other words related to the medical profession. Then encourage students to write a story using as many of these words as possible.

♦ *commercial*

Students may enjoy discussing commercials they have recently seen on television. Focus the discussion on how the commercials are designed to influence a person's buying habits.

♦ *constitution*

Extend the activity by having students check a dictionary to see how many different meanings they can find for the word *constitution.*

♦ *innocent*

Extend the activity by having students brainstorm in small groups to come up with lists of books and movies in which innocence or guilt is an important part of the plot. Encourage students to summarize the plot of each book or movie.

♦ This indicates a Unit Spelling Word.

Unit Activity Options

Challenge Yourself

You may want to extend the activity by having students number the blanks and write the missing words on a separate sheet of paper. Then they can trade papers with a classmate and review additional Spelling Words.

Suffix Scramble

Extend the exercise by having students create cards for additional words ending in *-ship*, *-ment*, or *-ity*. For example, some *-ment* words they might include are *government*, *encirclement*, *fragment*, *instrument*, and *ornament*.

Prefixes That Describe Where

Write the prefixes *de-* and *ex-* on the board. After students have read the introductory paragraph, lead them in a discussion of the meanings of the prefixes. After they have completed the activity, have volunteers read their responses aloud.

Spelling Check-Up

You may wish to create a fill-in-the-blank exercise of context sentences for words that cause most students problems. Distribute the sentences as a review.

Fantastic Folks

For this activity, place students in groups of four. After they have completed the game, encourage them to share their sayings with other groups.

Proofreading Partners

Encourage partners to discuss their ideas for paragraphs. Remind them that, to include the listed words, they may need to create an unusual or even a fantastic situation in their paragraphs.

Unit 4 Review *(continued)*

Curriculum Options

Language Arts: Name That *com-*

Divide the group into two teams with an extra person as a host. The host has twenty cards, each with a Spelling Word or another word that begins with the prefix *com-* or *con-* written on it. The host shows a card to one of the players on Team A and then puts it aside. That player must ask a question that calls for the word as its answer and then spell the word. (For example, if the host shows the word *commercial* to the player, the player might ask, "What do we call a TV advertisement?" and then spell the word.)

If the player spells the word correctly, Team A gets a point. If the player cannot ask a question that can be answered by the word or cannot spell the word correctly, a player from Team B gets a chance at the same word. If the player from Team B accomplishes the task, Team B gets the point. If not, Team A gets another turn, and so on. Teams take turns seeing each word first.

Language Arts: Who, What and Where?

This game is played with four students, two on each team. A fifth student is the host. The host has fifteen or twenty cards, each with a prepared question that can be answered with a word that ends in *-ance* or *-ence*. (Include words from students' lists and other words that end in one of these suffixes.) The host reads a question to one of the players on Team A. If the player guesses the word and spells it correctly, Team A gets a point. If the player guesses the wrong word, a player from Team B gets a chance to guess the word and spell it correctly. If he or she fails, Team A gets another turn, and so on. Teams take turns hearing each question first.

Social Studies: Who's Who?

Play this game in small groups, where each group competes against others to see which group can come up with the most historical tie-ins. Tell students to look at their Spelling Words and match them in a meaningful way with people famous for their activities in some field of endeavor.

Some tie-ins that students might make include Jane Goodall—friendship; Mikhail Gorbachev—leadership; Jackie Joyner-Kersee—championship; Robin Williams—personality; George Washington Carver—ability; and Mother Teresa—necessity. Tell students to be prepared to explain their tie-ins. For example, Mother Teresa provided basic necessities of life to people whom no one else wanted to help.

WHAT'S IN A WORD?

laid-back

Have students develop a list of synonyms for the word *laid-back*.

psychology

You may wish to extend this activity by having students think of other words using the Greek root *psych*. Some words they may list include *psychic, psychologist, psychiatrist,* and *psyche*.

raza

Students may enjoy listing all the ways they can think of for greeting friends and relatives. Some ways they may list include shaking hands, hugging, kissing on both cheeks, and slapping hands.

triumph

You may wish to extend this activity by having students think of ways in which triumphs have been celebrated throughout the ages. You may want to have students research such things as laurel wreaths, the Arc de Triomphe in Paris, Hollywood's Oscars, and the awarding of Olympic medals.

WORKING TOGETHER Students may enjoy writing and illustrating a class book on how people through the ages have celebrated triumphs.

transmutation

Students may enjoy learning that the process of trying to change common metals into gold or silver was called alchemy. Alchemy emerged in China and Egypt by the third century B.C. By the Middle Ages, it had made its way to Europe. Alchemists actually laid the groundwork for much chemistry as we know it today—which has, in fact, accomplished the transmutation of elements.

TEACHING STRATEGIES

Lesson 24: Patterns—More VCV Words

OBJECTIVE

To spell two-syllable words that contain a V/CV or a VC/V pattern

HOME ACTIVITY

The home activity is on page 147.

SECOND-LANGUAGE SUPPORT

Two-syllable words with a VCV pattern may have either a long or short vowel sound in the first syllable. Students whose first language is Vietnamese, Spanish, or Tagalog sometimes have difficulty differentiating between the long and short vowel sounds, as in *gate* and *get*. Have students brainstorm two-syllable words they know with the VCV pattern. Write the words on the board, and have volunteers underline the VCV patterns as they say the word aloud. COMPARING AND CONTRASTING

PRETEST/POSTTEST

1. The **prison** had strong locks on every door.
2. They washed the fine **linen** by hand.
3. The king and queen lived in a large **palace.**
4. The **climate** in the south is warmer than in the north.
5. The star of the show had a great deal of **talent.**
6. The **novel** was based on a true story.
7. The spy was put in jail for **treason.**
8. I read the **comic** strips in our newspaper.
9. We made a **profit** of ten dollars on the bake sale.
10. He sent a card as a **token** of friendship.
11. A rock can be a dangerous **weapon.**

(continued on next page)

Pretest

Administer the test on this page as a pretest. Say each word, use it in the sentence, and then repeat the word. ACCESSING PRIOR KNOWLEDGE

SELF-CHECK Have students check their own pretests against the list of Spelling Words. Remind students to write misspelled words in their Lesson Word Logs. STUDENT SELF-ASSESSMENT

Introducing the Lesson

Option A (Open Sort)

Distribute the word cards (page 146) to individuals or small groups, and guide them in an open-sort activity. In open sort, students group the word cards according to a criterion they select themselves. Then, guide students in comparing and discussing the criteria they selected.

Option B (Modeling)

Read aloud with students the lesson title and the Spelling Words. Use this model sentence to introduce the lesson skill in a context.

*The **spider finished** its web.*

Teaching the Lesson

- Ask volunteers to name the two-syllable words that have the VCV pattern with a long vowel sound in the first syllable, as in *titan*. As students name words, list them on the board. Then have students draw a line to show each division of syllables. *(climate, treason, token, gopher, siren, spiral)*
- Follow the same procedure with VCV words having a short vowel sound in the first syllable, as in *finish*. *(prison, palace, linen, talent, comic, profit, weapon, pleasant, novel, frigid)*
- After students have added words from their own writing to the columns, have volunteers read aloud all the words and underline each VCV pattern.

IN SUMMARY You may want students to summarize the lesson in their own words. Elicit from them that a two-syllable word with the VCV pattern may have either a long or a short vowel sound in the first syllable. If the pattern is V/CV, the sound is usually long; if the pattern is VC/V, the sound is usually short.

ASSIGNMENT Students can complete the first page of the lesson as a follow-up to the group activity, either in class or as homework.

Lesson 24: Patterns—More VCV Words *(continued)*

Practicing the Lesson

Spelling Clues: Classifying Errors

Encourage students to begin keeping track of the kinds of errors they make when they misspell a word. By noticing a pattern of errors, students can work to correct them.

Remind students that two-syllable words having the VCV pattern may have a long or a short vowel sound in the first syllable. Point out that the long *e* sound in *treason* and the short *e* sound in *pleasant* and *weapon* are spelled with two vowel letters (*ea*). Since *ea* spells one vowel sound, the pattern of the word is still VCV, not VVCV.

When students say a word with a long vowel in the first syllable, such as *token*, they should write the word as *to-ken* (V/CV). When they say a word with a short vowel in the first syllable, such as *novel*, they should write the word as *nov-el* (VC/V). Pronouncing each word while hearing the long or short vowel in the first syllable of the word can help students visualize the letters more easily. APPLYING SPELLING STRATEGIES

Proofreading

You may wish to have students review Spelling Clues: Classifying Errors before proofreading the paragraph.

Working with Meaning

Students may complete this activity individually or with a partner.

Posttest

Administer the test on page 54 as a posttest, or administer one of your own. Say each word, use it in a sentence, and then repeat the word.

Reteaching the Lesson

Students with auditory deficits will need more practice in segmenting words by ear and then applying the generalization to written words. Have students write all the Spelling Words with a long vowel sound in one column and all the words with a short vowel sound in another column. See whether students can apply inductive reasoning to come up with this generalization: Divide words that start with a long vowel sound after the first vowel sound, and divide words that start with a short vowel sound after the consonant following the vowel. AUDITORY MODALITY

(Pretest/Posttest, continued)

12. The **gopher** stuck its head out of the ground.
13. Today's weather is very **pleasant.**
14. The **siren** went off exactly at noon.
15. Snow and wind blew across the **frigid** tundra.
16. The stairs go upward in a **spiral.**

PRACTICE ACTIVITY

The practice activity is on page 148.

Answers: Spelling Clues

1. gopher
2. siren
3. spiral
4. token
5. treason
6. linen

Answers: Proofreading

7. talent
8. comic
9. prison
10. weapon
11. profit
12. palace

Answers: Working with Meaning

13. climate
14. frigid
15. pleasant
16. novel

Lesson 25: Mixed Spelling Patterns

OBJECTIVE

To spell two-syllable words having mixed spelling patterns

HOME ACTIVITY

The home activity is on page 150.

SECOND-LANGUAGE SUPPORT

Students whose first language is Vietnamese, Spanish, or Tagalog frequently have difficulty differentiating long and short vowel sounds. Help students to brainstorm words with mixed spelling patterns, and write them on the board. Have volunteers underline the vowel-consonant pattern in each word as they say the word aloud, stressing the long or short vowel sound in each syllable. COMPARING AND CONTRASTING

PRETEST/POSTTEST

1. We hung the **banner** on the wall.
2. How many people can stand safely on the **platform**?
3. The **hotel** had no empty rooms.
4. The water traveled through a **funnel.**
5. Are you in the **habit** of staying up late?
6. Many people stopped to look at the **display.**
7. The **clever** student solved the problem quickly.
8. How many apples can you **gather** in this bag?
9. The big room was **empty.**
10. No one knew what to do in the **chaos.**
11. The mystery story had a great deal of **suspense.**
12. **Saturn** is a planet in our solar system.
13. An ellipse is **oval.**
14. The **orphan** lived with a kind family.

(continued on next page)

Pretest

Administer the test on this page as a pretest. Say each word, use it in the sentence, and then repeat the word. ACCESSING PRIOR KNOWLEDGE

SELF-CHECK Have students check their own pretests against the list of Spelling Words. Remind students to write misspelled words in their Lesson Word Logs. STUDENT SELF-ASSESSMENT

Introducing the Lesson

Option A (Open Sort)

Distribute the word cards (page 149) to individuals or small groups, and guide them in an open-sort activity. In open sort, students group the word cards according to a criterion they select themselves. Then, guide students in comparing and discussing the criteria they selected.

Option B (Modeling)

Read aloud with students the lesson title and the Spelling Words. Use this model sentence to introduce the lesson skill in a context.

*We looked a **moment** at the **lavish** display.*

Teaching the Lesson

- Ask volunteers to name the two-syllable words that have the VC/CV pattern, as in *perform*. List the words on the board. Then have students draw a line to show each division of syllables. *(banner, funnel, suspense, orphan, crystal, platform)*
- Follow the same procedure with words having the pattern V/CV (as in *moment*), VC/V (as in *lavish*), VC/CCV (as in *disclose*), V/V (as in *fuel*), and VCC/CV (as in *campsite*). *(**V/CV:** hotel, oval, fatal; **VC/V:** habit, gather, Saturn, clever; **VC/CCV:** display; **V/V:** chaos; **VCC/CV:** empty)*
- After students have added words from their own writing to the columns, have volunteers read aloud all the words and underline each spelling pattern.

IN SUMMARY You may want students to summarize the lesson in their own words. Elicit from students that a word may be divided into syllables according to the pattern of vowel and consonant sounds.

ASSIGNMENT Students can complete the first page of the lesson as a follow-up to the group activity, either in class or as homework.

Lesson 25: Mixed Spelling Patterns *(continued)*

Practicing the Lesson

Spelling Clues: Writing Aloud

Suggest to students that when they say a word aloud, they focus on where the word is broken into syllables, based on its vowel-consonant spelling pattern. Breaking the word into syllables and saying each syllable aloud as they write it can aid them in the spelling of the entire word. Remind students that the *th* in *gather*, the *ph* in *orphan*, and the *pl* in *display* function as single consonant sounds.

Point out that hearing a long or a short vowel sound in the word's first syllable can serve as a hint to its syllabication. Words having a VC/CV or VC/V pattern frequently have a short vowel sound in the first syllable. Words having a V/CV or V/V pattern frequently have a long vowel sound in the first syllable. As students say each word pair aloud in the activity, have them tell where the word should be divided, based on the vowel sound heard in the first syllable. That can be used as a clue to choosing the word's correct spelling. APPLYING SPELLING STRATEGIES

Proofreading

You may wish to have students review Spelling Clues: Writing Aloud before proofreading the report.

Working with Meaning

Tell students to use the part of speech as a clue in completing each sentence. For example, the word in sentence 13 must be a noun, since the phrase is *The* _____; the word in sentence 15 must be a verb, since the phrase is *We could* _____. The Spelling Dictionary can be used to check definitions. PARTS OF SPEECH

Posttest

Administer the test on page 56 as a posttest, or administer one of your own. Say each word, use it in a sentence, and then repeat the word.

Reteaching the Lesson

Students with learning difficulties will need more practice in segmenting words and then applying the generalization. For each spelling pattern in this lesson, write the words on the board. Say each word, emphasizing the syllable division. Have students come to the board one at a time and draw a line to separate the words into syllables. See if students can apply inductive reasoning to state the generalization for dividing words. VISUAL MODALITY

(Pretest/Posttest, continued)

15. Everyone was sad after the **fatal** crash.

16. Light shone through the **crystal.**

PRACTICE ACTIVITY

The practice activity is on page 151.

Answers: Spelling Clues

1. orphan	**4.** chaos
2. hotel	**5.** funnel
3. habit	**6.** fatal

Answers: Proofreading

7. oval	**10.** banner
8. display	**11.** clever
9. platform	**12.** Saturn

Answers: Working with Meaning

13. crystal	**15.** gather
14. empty	**16.** suspense

Lesson 26: Unusual Plurals

OBJECTIVE

To spell words whose plural forms have unusual spellings

HOME ACTIVITY

The home activity is on page 153.

SECOND-LANGUAGE SUPPORT

Students with limited English proficiency may be confused by plurals with unusual endings, such as *-i, -a,* and *-ae,* or by collective nouns, such as *mice.* Have pictures available of singular and plural nouns, such as one *cactus* and two *cacti* or one *moose* and two *moose.* Write the appropriate singular and plural forms below each picture. Display the pictures in two columns on the wall, one labeled *Singular* and the other labeled *Plural.* Have students take turns reading the captions aloud. COMPARING AND CONTRASTING

PRETEST/POSTTEST

1. The **goldfish** swam in a large bowl.
2. We saw a rainbow **trout** in the lake.
3. All the **moose** crossed the road.
4. A **cactus** does not need much water to grow.
5. The news **media** gave lots of attention to the story.
6. Mushrooms are **fungi.**
7. Mouthwash helps kill **bacteria.**
8. The food was a **stimulus** for the animal to move.
9. What other **stimuli** do animals respond to besides food?
10. The eggs of some insects hatch to become **larvae.**
11. Do you know that the **radius** is a bone in your arm?
12. A **nucleus** is the central core of an atom.
13. The **nuclei** of all atoms carry a positive electrical charge.

(continued on next page)

Pretest

Administer the test on this page as a pretest. Say each word, use it in the sentence, and then repeat the word. ACCESSING PRIOR KNOWLEDGE

SELF-CHECK Have students check their own pretests against the list of Spelling Words. Remind students to write misspelled words in their Lesson Word Logs. STUDENT SELF-ASSESSMENT

Introducing the Lesson

Option A (Open Sort)

Distribute the word cards (page 152) to individuals or small groups, and guide them in an open-sort activity. In open sort, students group the word cards according to a criterion they select themselves. Then, guide students in comparing and discussing the criteria they selected.

Option B (Modeling)

Read aloud with students the lesson title and the Spelling Words. Use this model sentence to introduce the lesson skill in a context.

*Each **alumnus** joined the **alumni** club.*

Teaching the Lesson

- Ask volunteers to name and spell the Spelling Words that are singular nouns ending in *-us,* and write them on the board under the heading *octopus. (cactus, stimulus, radius, nucleus, hippopotamus)*
- Follow the same procedure for Spelling Words that are plural nouns ending in *-a* or *-ae,* and *-i.* (**-*a* or -*ae*:** *media, bacteria, larvae;* **-*i*:** *fungi, stimuli, nuclei)*
- Follow the same procedure with collective nouns. Point out that the form for each of these nouns is the same for singular or plural. *(goldfish, trout, moose, species, salmon)*
- After students have added words from their own writing to the columns, have volunteers underline each singular or plural ending, where appropriate.

IN SUMMARY You may want students to summarize the lesson in their own words. Elicit from students that the plural form of singular nouns ending in *-us* is usually *-i.* Some plurals end in *-a* or *-ae.* Other words have the same singular and plural form.

ASSIGNMENT Students can complete the first page of the lesson as a follow-up to the group activity, either in class or as homework.

Lesson 26: Unusual Plurals *(continued)*

Practicing the Lesson

Spelling Clues: Word Shapes

Suggest to students that before they write a word, they close their eyes and try to picture the word in their minds. After determining the letters they "see," they should write those letters on paper.

Students might be curious about some of the corresponding singular or plural forms that are not given for the Spelling Words in this lesson. Tell students the endings are based on Latin and follow these patterns.

- Singular nouns ending in *-us* frequently take an *-i* ending to form the plural (for example, *cactus/cacti, radius/radii,* and *nucleus/nuclei*). However, the plural of many of the same *-us* words may also be correctly spelled with an *-es* ending *(cactuses, radiuses, nucleuses).*
- Conversely, the singular form of plurals ending in *-i* usually ends in *-us* (for example, *fungus, stimulus,* and *nucleus*).
- The singular forms of *media* and *bacteria* are *medium* and *bacterium.* The singular form of *larvae* is *larva.* APPLYING SPELLING STRATEGIES

Proofreading

You may wish to have students review Spelling Clues: Word Shapes before proofreading the paragraph.

Fun with Words

Students may complete this activity individually or with a partner. Point out that some of the answers are in singular form *(nucleus, hippopotamus, cactus),* some are in plural form *(nuclei, larvae),* and one may be either form *(salmon).*

Posttest

Administer the test on page 58 as a posttest, or administer one of your own. Say each word, use it in a sentence, and then repeat the word.

Reteaching the Lesson

Create a chart with three columns, one headed *Singular,* one headed *Plural,* and one headed *Either.* Have students write each Spelling Word in the appropriate column. After each Spelling Word has been written, have students write the corresponding singular or plural form for each word. For example, for the word *cactus* in the *Singular* column, students should write *cacti* in the *Plural* column. Encourage students to use the dictionary when they are unsure of the singular or the plural form of a word. VISUAL MODALITY

(Pretest/Posttest, continued)

14. How many different **species** of plants and animals are there?

15. The **salmon** swam up the stream.

16. A **hippopotamus** is a very heavy animal.

PRACTICE ACTIVITY

The practice activity is on page 154.

Answers: Spelling Clues

1. moose **3.** stimuli
2. trout **4.** species

Answers: Proofreading

5. goldfish **8.** bacteria
6. stimulus **9.** fungi
7. media **10.** radius

Answers: Fun with Words

11. salmon **14.** larvae
12. nucleus **15.** hippopotamus
13. nuclei **16.** cactus

Lesson 27: Adjective Suffixes *-ive, -ous*

OBJECTIVE

To spell adjectives having an *-ive* or *-ous* suffix

HOME ACTIVITY

The home activity is on page 156.

SECOND-LANGUAGE SUPPORT

Students for whom English is not a first language may be confused by words having an *-ive* suffix. Explain that some English words have an *-ive* ending that is not a suffix, as in *give* or *live*. Words whose *-ive* ending is a suffix often have a recognizable base word. For example, the base word of *attractive* is *attract*; the base word of *creative* is *create*. COMPARING AND CONTRASTING

PRETEST/POSTTEST

1. Always try to see things in a **positive** way.
2. A movie star is often an **attractive** person.
3. The new rule proved to be very **effective.**
4. The class likes books on **various** topics.
5. Are you **curious** about what is in the box?
6. A **tremendous** wind nearly blew my hat off.
7. The elephant is an **enormous** animal.
8. The answer to the problem is **obvious.**
9. I ate a **delicious** meal.
10. That person is acting in a **mysterious** way.
11. The **executive** board voted to accept the lowest bid.
12. People who write songs must be **creative.**
13. You did a **fabulous** job at the meeting.
14. The **legislative** branch makes the laws.

(continued on next page)

Pretest

Administer the test on this page as a pretest. Say each word, use it in the sentence, and then repeat the word. ACCESSING PRIOR KNOWLEDGE

SELF-CHECK Have students check their own pretests against the list of Spelling Words. Remind students to write misspelled words in their Lesson Word Logs. STUDENT SELF-ASSESSMENT

Introducing the Lesson

Option A (Open Sort)

Distribute the word cards (page 155) to individuals or small groups, and guide them in an open-sort activity. In open sort, students group the word cards according to a criterion they select themselves. Then, guide students in comparing and discussing the criteria they selected.

Option B (Modeling)

Read aloud with students the lesson title and the Spelling Words. Use this model sentence to introduce the lesson skill in a context.

*The baby is an **active** and **precious** child.*

Teaching the Lesson

- Write the word *massive* on the board. As volunteers name the words that have the *-ive* suffix, list the words on the board under *massive*. *(positive, attractive, effective, executive, creative, legislative, negative, sensitive)*
- Follow the same procedure with words having the suffix *-ous*. Have students choose a Spelling Word as a heading for the list. *(various, curious, tremendous, enormous, obvious, delicious, mysterious, fabulous)*
- After students have added words from their own writing to the columns, have volunteers read aloud all the words and underline each suffix.

IN SUMMARY You may want students to summarize the lesson in their own words. Elicit from students that if a base word ends with *e*, the *e* must be dropped before adding *-ive* or *-ous*; if a base word ends in a consonant and *y*, *y* must be changed to *i* before adding *-ous*. These rules can be used to spell an unfamiliar adjective that ends with *-ive* or *-ous*.

ASSIGNMENT Students can complete the first page of the lesson as a follow-up to the group activity, either in class or as homework.

Lesson 27: Adjective Suffixes *-ive, -ous* (continued)

Practicing the Lesson

Spelling Clues: Find the Base Word

Suggest to students that they begin each item by writing the base word. For example, they should write *mystery* before deciding whether *misterious* or *mysterious* is correct. The first *y* in *mystery* will tell them that *mysterious* is the correct spelling.

Remind students of these rules for changing a base word to a word with a suffix.

If the base word ends in *e*, the *e* is dropped before the addition of *-ive* or *-ous*.

create —> creative

If a base word ends in a consonant and *y*, the *y* changes to *i* before the addition of *-ous*.

vary —> various

Remind students that words ending with *-ive* or *-ous* are adjectives. APPLYING SPELLING STRATEGIES

Proofreading

You may wish to have students review Spelling Clues: Find the Base Word before proofreading the sentences.

Working with Meaning

Students may complete this activity individually or with a partner. Tell them not to use Spelling Words already used in items 1–12.

SECOND-LANGUAGE SUPPORT Have students work with a partner to complete the activity. Encourage students to express the meaning of each sentence in their own words.

Posttest

Administer the test on page 60 as a posttest, or administer one of your own. Say each word, use it in a sentence, and then repeat the word.

Reteaching the Lesson

Students with visual memory deficits may need additional practice in writing word endings. Have these students follow these steps:

1. Write the base word plus the suffix. For example: attract + ive = attractive
2. Trace the word, using a colored pen.
3. In pencil, copy the word beneath the model, saying each letter as it is written.
4. Cover the model and write the word from recall. VISUAL/KINESTHETIC MODALITIES

(Pretest/Posttest, continued)

15. You won't get far with a **negative** attitude.
16. Try to be **sensitive** to the feelings of others.

PRACTICE ACTIVITY

The practice activity is on page 157.

Answers: Spelling Clues

1. mysterious
2. various
3. legislative
4. effective
5. attractive
6. creative

Answers: Proofreading

7. fabulous
8. sensitive
9. delicious
10. tremendous
11. curious
12. enormous

Answers: Working with Meaning

13. executive
14. positive
15. negative
16. obvious

Lesson 28: Words with Prefixes/Suffixes

OBJECTIVE

To spell words with both a prefix and a suffix

HOME ACTIVITY

The home activity is on page 159.

SECOND-LANGUAGE SUPPORT

Students for whom English is not the first language may be confused by certain prefixes or suffixes. Make clear that letter groups are not considered prefixes unless a base word follows. For example, *read* does not begin with the prefix *re-*. Likewise, suffixes must follow a base word or root. Words such as *table* and *lion* do not have suffixes even though they end with the letter groups *able* and *ion*. COMPARING AND CONTRASTING

PRETEST/POSTTEST

1. It is **unlikely** that it will snow in the summer.
2. The **repayment** of the loan was on time.
3. My **reaction** to the news was one of shock.
4. They quickly found a **replacement** for the worker who left.
5. A new pet may act in **unpredictable** ways.
6. The boys did not talk to each other after their **disagreement.**
7. Will there be a **renewal** of my contract?
8. One of our biggest problems is **unemployment.**
9. I **unexpectedly** won first prize.
10. We **unfortunately** missed the bus by one minute.
11. It seems **unusually** hot today.
12. The artist made a **reproduction** of her painting.
13. They began the **reconstruction** of their home after the flood.

(continued on next page)

Pretest

Administer the test on this page as a pretest. Say each word, use it in the sentence, and then repeat the word. ACCESSING PRIOR KNOWLEDGE

SELF-CHECK Have students check their own pretests against the list of Spelling Words. Remind students to write misspelled words in their Lesson Word Logs. STUDENT SELF-ASSESSMENT

Introducing the Lesson

Option A (Open Sort)

Distribute the word cards (page 158) to individuals or small groups, and guide them in an open-sort activity. In open sort, students group the word cards according to a criterion they select themselves. Then, guide students in comparing and discussing the criteria they selected.

Option B (Modeling)

Read aloud with students the lesson title and the Spelling Words. Use this model sentence to introduce the lesson skill in a context.

*Her **restatement** of the answer was **unacceptable.***

Teaching the Lesson

- Ask volunteers to name the Spelling Words having the prefix *un-*. List the words on the board. Have students underline the prefix and suffix in each word. Point out that these prefixes and suffixes do not change the spelling of the base word. *(unlikely, unpredictable, unemployment, unexpectedly, unfortunately, unusually, unsuccessful, uncomfortable)*
- Follow the same procedure with words having the prefixes *re-* and *dis-*. (**re-:** *repayment, reaction, replacement, renewal, reproduction, reconstruction;* **dis-:** *disagreement, disagreeable)*
- Have students add words from their own writing to columns. (These words may include instances where the spelling of the base changes.

IN SUMMARY You may want students to summarize the lesson. Elicit that the prefixes *un-*, *re-*, and *dis-* change the meaning of a word but not the spelling of the base word. The suffixes *-able*, *-ly*, *-ment*, *-al*, *-ful*, and *-ion* change the word's meaning and, sometimes, the spelling of the base word.

ASSIGNMENT Students can complete the first page of the lesson as a follow-up to the group activity, either in class or as homework.

Lesson 28: Words with Prefixes/Suffixes *(continued)*

Practicing the Lesson

Spelling Clues: Prefixes and Suffixes

Suggest to students that when they search for a base word, they first look to see if the word has a prefix and then write the word without the prefix. Next, they should find the word's suffix and write the word without its suffix.

Remind students that sometimes the spelling of a base word changes when a suffix is added, especially if the base word ends in *e* or a consonant and *y*. APPLYING SPELLING STRATEGIES

Proofreading

You may wish to have students review Spelling Clues: Prefixes and Suffixes before proofreading the note.

Working with Meaning

Students may complete this activity individually or with a partner. Tell them not to use Spelling Words they have already used in items 1–12. Have them use context clues to tell whether the word required is an adjective *(disagreeable, uncomfortable)* or a noun *(disagreement, reconstruction).* The Spelling Dictionary can be used to check definitions.

SECOND-LANGUAGE SUPPORT Have students work with a partner. After reading each sentence aloud, students should explain the meaning of the Spelling Word that was used. For example, the student might say, "*Disagreeable* means 'not able to agree with.'" WORD MEANINGS

Posttest

Administer the test on page 62 as a posttest, or administer one of your own. Say each word, use it in a sentence, and then repeat the word.

Reteaching the Lesson

The following strategy can help students with learning difficulties spell words with prefixes and suffixes. Write the prefixes *re-*, *un-* , and *dis-* on cards. Then write the suffixes *-able, -ment, -ly, -al, -ful,* and *-ion* on other cards. List the base word of each Spelling Word on the board. Then have students find cards with a prefix and suffix that can be added to the base word. Have students hold up the cards beside the words. Have the student spell the Spelling Word aloud as other students write the word on their papers. KINESTHETIC MODALITY

(Pretest/Posttest, continued)

14. I don't get along with **disagreeable** people.
15. We were **unsuccessful** in trying to find the lost ball.
16. Are you **uncomfortable** sleeping without a pillow?

PRACTICE ACTIVITY

The practice activity is on page 160.

Answers: Spelling Clues

1. unsuccessful
2. unusually
3. renewal
4. reaction
5. repayment
6. reconstruction

Answers: Proofreading

7. unfortunately
8. reproduction
9. unpredictable
10. unusually
11. unlikely
12. unemployment

Answers: Working with Meaning

13. disagreeable
14. uncomfortable
15. disagreement
16. replacement

Unit 5 Review

OBJECTIVES

- To review spelling patterns and strategies in Lessons 24–28
- To give students the opportunity to recognize and use these spelling patterns and Spelling Words in their writing

UNIT 5 WORDS

The following words are reviewed in Practice Test, Parts A and B.

Lesson 24: Patterns—More VCV Words

profit	talent
pleasant	palace

Lesson 25: Mixed Spelling Patterns

banner	clever
crystal	

Lesson 26: Unusual Plurals

salmon	bacteria
radius	fungi
species	

Lesson 27: Adjective Suffixes *-ive, -ous*

delicious	curious
attractive	enormous

Lesson 28: Words with Prefixes/Suffixes

replacement	unsuccessful
unpredictable	disagreement

Review Strategies

Review with students the following spelling-clue strategies for Lessons 24–28.

Lesson 24 Spelling Clues: Classifying Errors

Tell students to write the words *weapon, pleasant,* and *talent* on a sheet of paper. Have volunteers place different responses on the board (*wepon* or *weapon, pleasent* or *pleasant,* for example). Circle common spelling errors that form a pattern (using *e* for *ea,* or *ent* for *ant,* for example). Remind students that keeping track of the kinds of errors they make can help them avoid making the same mistakes again.

Lesson 25 Spelling Clues: Writing Aloud

Tell students to listen carefully. Say the word *chaos.* Ask students to suggest how the word might be spelled. Write the responses (*kayos* and *chaos,* for example) on the board. Have the class decide on the correct spelling. Point out that saying a word aloud and listening to its sounds can help in spelling an unfamiliar word.

Lesson 26 Spelling Clues: Word Shapes

Write the word *hippopotamus* on the board. Ask volunteers to identify the tallest letters, or ascenders (*h* and *t*). Then have them identify the lowest letters, or descenders (three *p*'s). Remind students that remembering the shapes of the letters in a word can help them spell the word correctly.

Lesson 27 Spelling Clues: Find the Base Word

Write the word *mystery* on the board. Then ask a volunteer to write the word *mysterious* next to it. Have a volunteer explain how the base word changed. (The *y* was dropped before the suffix was added.) Remind students that the addition of suffixes does not always alter the spelling of a base word.

Lesson 28 Spelling Clues: Prefixes and Suffixes

Write the word *uncomfortable* on the board. Have students identify the prefix and suffix and tell whether the base word underwent any change when the affixes were added (no). Remind students that the addition of prefixes and suffixes does not always alter the spelling of a base word.

Unit 5 Review *(continued)*

Practice Test

The Practice Test provides an opportunity to review Spelling Words and spelling generalizations in a standardized test format, complete with a sample answer card.

Option 1

Use Practice Test: Part A as a pretest. Later, use Practice Test: Part B as a posttest.

Option 2

Have students review their Lesson Word Log for this unit. If they need extra help, you may wish to review the spelling generalizations discussed in the individual lessons. Then administer both parts of the Practice Test to determine whether students have mastered the spelling generalizations.

Practice Test: Part A

1. (B) palice [palace]
2. (B) samon [salmon]
3. (C) profet [profit]
4. (A) delishius [delicious]
5. (A) bannar [banner]
6. (D) atractive [attractive]
7. (D) chrystal [crystal]
8. (B) replacment [replacement]
9. (D) radias [radius]
10. (A) pleasent [pleasant]

Practice Test: Part B

1. (D) curious
2. (B) clever
3. (D) talent
4. (C) enormous
5. (B) species
6. (C) bacteria
7. (A) fungi
8. (B) unpredictable
9. (C) unsuccessful
10. (A) disagreement

Options for Evaluation

- Have students check their own Practice Tests against their lists of Spelling Words. The list on the opposite page provides references to the lessons where they can find words they misspelled.
- You may prefer to assign partners and have students check each other's Practice Tests, using their own list of Spelling Words.

REVIEW ACTIVITIES

Activity 1

Group students in threes or fours to play a spelling game using the words from this review lesson. The first player chooses a word and says its first letter aloud, and the next player says the next letter. Play continues until the last letter is given. The player who gives the last letter is the winner of that round.

Activity 2

For students who need a reteaching activity, have them write the words from this review lesson on individual index cards. Mix the cards together, and then have students arrange all the cards in alphabetical order. Let a student choose a card from the pile, say the word aloud, and spell it. Then have the student draw another card, read the word aloud, and have another student tell whether the second word comes before or after the first one alphabetically. Let a volunteer spell the second word and then draw a new card from the pile to play another round.

Activity 3

If students use computers, you may wish to show them how the computer can help them locate and correct words they have misspelled. Encourage students to check to see if the words from this review lesson are already entered in the computer's memory. If not, help students enter them as part of the computer's spelling word list.

Unit 5 Review *(continued)*

WHAT'S IN A WORD?

♦ *media*

Have students list genres of media programs (talk show, for example). Students might also list actual names of media programs from radio or TV or list names of newspapers and magazines.

palace

Encourage students to name other words they know that are related to the word *palace.* Students may mention *palatial.* (Point out that the word *palladium* has a different source, named for the Greek goddess Pallas Athena.) Also have students look up the words *palatine* and *paladin* to find their connection to the word *palace.*

sensitive

Encourage students to list words that are related to *sensitive.* Additional words might include *senseless, sensationalism, sensitivity, sensitize, sensor, sensory,* and *sensuous.* Encourage students to use their words in original sentences.

♦ This indicates a Unit Spelling Word.

Unit Activity Options

Round Robin

Appoint one group member to read the entire story aloud once all the sentences have been contributed. Members of the group may take turns spelling aloud the Spelling Word in each sentence.

Suspenseful Titles

Suggest that students look at the titles they listed in the *What's in a Word?* activity about the word *suspense* before writing their own.

Select Some Words

As an extension activity, have students take a class survey to discover which Spelling Words they feel are most difficult to spell. Students can present the survey results by making a long list of Spelling Words in order of difficulty, based on classmates' answers.

Your Own Usage Notes

As a variant activity, have each pair of students find another pair and write a short story using all eight words from the new group.

Play Charades

Suggest to students that they use newspaper and magazine articles about sports events to find interesting action words to write on their cards. To make the game more challenging, you may wish to limit the number of guesses group members can take before the answer is revealed.

Story Dictation

Students may wish to build a story by having one student contribute one sentence, a second student contribute another sentence, and so on. The last student must provide a conclusion for the story.

Proofreading Partners

Encourage partners to discuss their ideas for paragraphs. Remind them that, to include the listed words, they may need to create an unusual or even a fantastic situation in their paragraphs.

Unit 5 Review *(continued)*

Curriculum Options

Language Arts: Prefix/Suffix Word Building

Have students prepare index cards with a different prefix or suffix from the lesson on each card. Then have them write a number of base words, chosen at random, on other individual index cards. Students shuffle all the prefix and suffix cards and place them in a single pile face down. They shuffle all the base words and place them in another pile face down.

Pair students to play a card game using the two piles of cards. Player A turns over one card from the prefix/suffix pile and one card from the base word pile. The player then says and writes down as many words as he or she is able, using the prefix or the suffix along with the base word. The cards are then placed at the bottoms of the piles, and player B draws two new cards and follows the same procedure. If a base word cannot be combined with the prefix or suffix, the play goes to the next player. The winner is the player who has made more words by the end of the game.

Music: Music Syllables

Organize students in small groups. Distribute sheet music to each group. Call attention to the way the words, or song lyrics, frequently are hyphenated to show how each syllable is sung to a different musical note. Have group members write down each word that is hyphenated in the sheet music and then group the words according to these spelling patterns: VC/CV, V/CV, VC/V, V/V, and VCC/CV.

Science: Word Search

Remind students that many words with an unusual plural form are words related to science, such as *bacteria, larvae, fungi, stimuli,* and *nuclei.* Organize students in small groups, and give each group a science textbook or another science reference. Give group members time to peruse the contents of their reference book to locate examples of plural words with unusual spellings. Assign a Recorder to each group to write down examples that each group finds. Later, have group members list the unusual plurals on the board. As an additional activity, students can determine the singular form of each plural found and make a separate list of these spellings as well.

WHAT'S IN A WORD?

suspense

Have students list titles of suspense programs or movies. You may wish to supply students with old television guides or names of movie titles, which students can use to brainstorm titles of suspense.

♦ talent

Students may wish to think of other words related to *talent (gift, aptitude, faculty, knack, genius)* and research the differences among them.

unpredictable/dictionary

Encourage students to explain the connection between the words *unpredictable* and *dictionary* and the idea of "to speak." Stress that to predict means "to speak about a future event," and that the dictionary tells you how to speak, or say, a word.

♦ This indicates a Unit Spelling Word.

Lesson 30: Suffixes in Combination

OBJECTIVE

To spell words that have two suffixes

HOME ACTIVITY

The home activity is on page 162.

SECOND-LANGUAGE SUPPORT

Spanish-speaking students may find it hard to hear the final *p* (as in *ownership* and *relationship*), because neither the final sound of *p* nor the final sound of *b* occurs often in Spanish. Begin by giving students practice in repeating groups of words like the following and underlining the consonants that spell the final sounds: *mop/mob; cap/cab; lap/lab; cop/cob;* and *rip/rib.* Then have students identify Spelling Words that have a final *p* sound. MAKING SOUND-LETTER CORRESPONDENCES

PRETEST/POSTTEST

1. Tim **carefully** carried the dishes to the kitchen.
2. Pet **ownership** is a serious responsibility.
3. Loretta stuck **faithfully** to her beliefs.
4. Many Native Americans lived **peacefully** beside the new settlers.
5. She performed that flute solo **wonderfully.**
6. Each morning Rob **thoughtfully** clears the breakfast table.
7. Gina has a very good **relationship** with her parents.
8. Tokyo and Washington, D.C., **respectively,** are the capitals of Japan and the United States.
9. This trail mix is sweetened **naturally** with dried fruit.
10. Jerry waited **nervously** for his name to be called.
11. The young skater glides **gracefully** over the ice.

(continued on next page)

Pretest

Administer the test on this page as a pretest. Say each word, use it in the sentence, and then repeat the word. ACCESSING PRIOR KNOWLEDGE

SELF-CHECK Have students check their own pretests against the list of Spelling Words. Remind students to write misspelled words in their Lesson Word Logs. STUDENT SELF-ASSESSMENT

Introducing the Lesson

Option A (Open Sort)

Distribute the word cards (page 161) to individuals or small groups, and guide them in an open-sort activity. In open sort, students group the word cards according to a criterion they select themselves. Then, guide students in comparing and discussing the criteria they selected.

Option B (Modeling)

Read aloud with students the lesson title and the Spelling Words. Use this model sentence to introduce the lesson skill in a context.

Incidentally, that was the choir singing *joyously.*

Teaching the Lesson

- Ask volunteers to name some Spelling Words that have the same two suffixes as in *fearfully*. List the words on the board. Then have volunteers circle each suffix. *(carefully, faithfully, peacefully, wonderfully, thoughtfully, gracefully, joyfully, beautifully, successfully)*
- Follow the same procedure for the other Spelling Words that end in *-ly*. *(respectively, naturally, nervously, actively, accidentally)*
- Follow the same procedure for words that end with the suffix *-ship*. *(ownership, relationship)*
- After students have added words from their own reading or writing to the columns, have volunteers read aloud all the words and identify the suffixes.

IN SUMMARY You may want students to summarize the lesson in their own words.

Elicit from students that when a suffix is added to a base word, sometimes the spelling of the base word changes.

ASSIGNMENT Students can complete the first page of the lesson as a follow-up to the group activity, either in class or as homework.

Lesson 30: Suffixes in Combination *(continued)*

Practicing the Lesson

Spelling Clues: Suffixes

Remind students that when a suffix is added to a word, the spelling of the base word may change. See if they can pinpoint the part of the base word that normally changes (the end of the base word). Provide examples. You may point out that *nature* changes to *natur* before the suffix *-al* is added to form the word *natural*, and that *beauty* changes to *beauti* before the suffix *-ful* is added. Changes do not normally occur near the beginning of the word. For example, *oarsmanship* would not change to *orsmanship* or *oursmanship*. Tell students to keep these guidelines in mind as they check the spellings of the words in the activity. Have students complete the activity independently or in pairs. APPLYING SPELLING STRATEGIES

TRANSITIONAL SPELLERS Have students use slash marks to divide the words into base word, first suffix, and final suffix. Tell students to keep these guidelines in mind as they check the spelling of one word part at a time. Remind them that in some base words an *e* may be dropped or a *y* changed to *i* before the first suffix is added.

Proofreading

You may wish to have students review Spelling Clues: Suffixes before proofreading the sentences.

Fun with Words

Have students complete the activity with Spelling Words they have not already written on lines 1–12. You may want to have students write other *-ly* words that could be illustrated by the pictures. Words students list may include *sloppily, intentionally, cordially, nervously, tentatively*, and *mentally*.

Posttest

Administer the test on page 68 as a posttest, or administer one of your own. Say each word, use it in a sentence, and then repeat the word.

Reteaching the Lesson

Write these suffixes on cards: *-ful, -ly, -ive, -ous, -al, -er, -ship,* and *-ion*. Have students write the Spelling Words on cards, omitting either the first or the second suffix (for example: *natur_____ly, owner_____*). Students should place their cards face down in a pile. Then have students draw a card from the pile, match it with the correct suffix card, and spell the word. KINESTHETIC MODALITY

(Pretest/Posttest, continued)

12. The children played **actively** all morning.

13. The choir sang **joyfully.**

14. Georgia painted the sunset **beautifully.**

15. The Panthers **successfully** ended the season with a victory.

16. I broke the window **accidentally.**

PRACTICE ACTIVITY

The practice activity is on page 163.

Answers: Spelling Clues

1. relationship	**4.** faithfully
2. joyfully	**5.** naturally
3. ownership	**6.** actively

Answers: Proofreading

7. nervously	**10.** gracefully
8. successfully	**11.** carefully
9. beautifully	**12.** wonderfully

Answers: Fun with Words

13. accidentally	**15.** respectively
14. peacefully	**16.** thoughtfully

Lesson 31: Prefix *in- (im-, il-, ir-)*

OBJECTIVE

To spell words that include one of these variations of the prefix *in-: im-, il-, ir-*

HOME ACTIVITY

The home activity is on page 165.

SECOND-LANGUAGE SUPPORT

Speakers of Chinese, Vietnamese, Tagalog, and Spanish often confuse the short *i* sound with the long *e* sound. Write the words *sit* and *seat* on the board. Pronounce each word and underline the letters that make the vowel sound. Then write these pairs of words on the board: *did/deed*; *grin/green*; *bin/bean*; and *dim/deem*. Have volunteers pronounce the words and underline the letters that spell the vowel sounds. MAKING SOUND-LETTER CORRESPONDENCES

PRETEST/POSTTEST

1. Your homework is **incomplete.**
2. Mom and Dad had an **informal** dinner party last week.
3. You have only two **incorrect** answers.
4. Angie felt quite **independent** after she moved out.
5. Fireworks are **illegal** in many cities.
6. Most people think it's **impolite** to talk with your mouth full.
7. Charles says it's **impossible** to clone dinosaurs from fossils.
8. The wizard made himself **invisible** before he entered the castle.
9. These **irregular** puzzle pieces must be connectors of some kind.
10. Camping can be enjoyable and **inexpensive.**
11. They couldn't drink the water because it was **impure.**
12. Her **inability** to shoot baskets kept her off the team.

(continued on next page)

Pretest

Administer the test on this page as a pretest. Say each word, use it in the sentence, and then repeat the word. ACCESSING PRIOR KNOWLEDGE

SELF-CHECK Have students check their own pretests against the list of Spelling Words. Remind students to write misspelled words in their Lesson Word Logs. STUDENT SELF-ASSESSMENT

Introducing the Lesson

Option A (Open Sort)

Distribute the word cards (page 164) to individuals or small groups, and guide them in an open-sort activity. In open sort, students group the word cards according to a criterion they select themselves. Then, guide students in comparing and discussing the criteria they selected.

Option B (Modeling)

Read aloud with students the lesson title and the Spelling Words. Use this model sentence to introduce the lesson skill in a context.

*It's **illogical** for this machine to produce an **inappropriate** widget.*

Teaching the Lesson

- Tell students that the prefix *in-* usually means "not" and appears as *in-*, *im-*, *il-* or *ir-*. Ask volunteers to name Spelling Words in which the prefix has the form it has in *indirect*. List them on the board under the heading *indirect*. *(incomplete, informal, incorrect, independent, invisible, inexpensive, inability, indigestion, indefinite, incredible)*
- Follow the same procedure for the words beginning with *im-*, *ir-*, and *il-*. You might want to head one column with *impersonal* and have students suggest headings for the other two columns. *(**im-:** impolite, impossible, impure, impatient; **il-:** illegal; **ir-:** irregular)*
- After students have added words from their own reading or writing to the columns, call on volunteers to read the words and underline the prefixes.

IN SUMMARY Encourage students to summarize the lesson in their own words. Elicit from students the fact that the prefix *in-* may appear as *in-*, *im-*, *il-*, or *ir-*, and that this prefix does not change the spelling of the base word.

ASSIGNMENT Students can complete the first page of the lesson as a follow-up to the group activity, either in class or as homework.

Lesson 31: Prefix *in- (im-, il-, ir-)* *(continued)*

Practicing the Lesson

Spelling Clues: Visual Clues

Tell students that one way to check for correct spelling is to write the word and see if the word looks right. If it doesn't, tell them to keep trying until it does. If they still aren't sure, tell them to look up the word in a dictionary or use the spell-check program on their computers.

Remind students that another way to look at a word is to break the word into prefix and base word and then check the spelling of each part. Work through an example or two with students before assigning the activity. The following Spelling Words exemplify the process well: ir + regular, il + legal.

Ask students why they think the variants *ir-* and *il-* are used in some words. (They precede words beginning with *r* and *l*.) APPLYING SPELLING STRATEGIES

Proofreading

You may wish to have students review Spelling Clues: Visual Clues before proofreading the letter.

Working with Meaning

If students have trouble with this activity, tell them to drop the prefix from the word and choose a base word that means exactly the same as the definition. ANTONYMS

Posttest

Administer the test on page 70 as a posttest, or administer one of your own. Say each word, use it in a sentence, and then repeat the word.

Reteaching the Lesson

Some students use the first option that comes to mind (such as trying to remember a spelling) rather than applying an effective spelling strategy (such as dividing a word into syllables). Teach these students to use "self-interrogation." Have the student ask himself or herself questions like these while spelling a word: *Can I divide this word into syllables? What's the first sound I hear in the second syllable? What letter or letter combinations represent the last sound I hear in the word?*

Have students divide the words into syllables, say the words aloud, and check that there is a vowel in each syllable. Check their syllable breaks. Then dictate the words to students and have them spell the words on paper one syllable at a time. AUDITORY MODALITY

(Pretest/Posttest, continued)

13. The coach became **impatient** with the team's lack of interest.
14. Do bell peppers give you **indigestion?**
15. The store will be closed for an **indefinite** period.
16. It's **incredible** that people have climbed to the top of Mt. Everest.

PRACTICE ACTIVITY

The practice activity is on page 166.

Answers: Spelling Clues

1. illegal
2. impossible
3. impatient
4. incorrect
5. independent
6. informal

Answers: Proofreading

7. incredible
8. inexpensive
9. inability
10. indigestion
11. impolite
12. incomplete

Answers: Working with Meaning

13. impure
14. indefinite
15. invisible
16. irregular

Lesson 32: Roots *-scrib-/-script-*, *-spect-*

OBJECTIVE

To spell words with the Latin roots *-scrib-/-script-* or *-spect-*

HOME ACTIVITY

The home activity is on page 168.

SECOND-LANGUAGE SUPPORT

The consonant cluster *scr* may be difficult for those from several language backgrounds. Write *scram, scam, cam,* and *crew* on the board. Read the words aloud, emphasizing the initial sounds. Then, as you read each of the following words aloud, have students come to the board and point to the word that has the same beginning sound: *skunk, scream, cream, cat, skip, script, skirt, cry, scale, scribe, come, scribbled, cross, crane,* and *skin.* MAKING SOUND-LETTER CORRESPONDENCES

PRETEST/POSTTEST

1. I'm going to **inspect** your room in five minutes.
2. I **suspect** you forgot to study.
3. The **scribe** was an important recordkeeper in ages past.
4. May I have a copy of the **script** so I can learn my lines?
5. The words you chose are very **descriptive.**
6. The witness gave a **description** of the suspect to the police.
7. The doctor **prescribed** a cream for the baby's rash.
8. The **inspector** says the hurricane made the building unsafe.
9. Fireworks create quite a **spectacle.**
10. The laser light show was **spectacular.**
11. My little sister **scribbled** on my homework.
12. Can you read the tiny **inscription** on the tablet?

(continued on next page)

Pretest

Administer the test on this page as a pretest. Say each word, use it in the sentence, and then repeat the word. ACCESSING PRIOR KNOWLEDGE

SELF-CHECK Have students check their own pretests against the list of Spelling Words. Remind students to write misspelled words in their Lesson Word Logs. STUDENT SELF-ASSESSMENT

Introducing the Lesson

Option A (Open Sort)

Distribute the word cards (page 167) to individuals or small groups, and guide them in an open-sort activity. In open sort, students group the word cards according to a criterion they select themselves. Then, guide students in comparing and discussing the criteria they selected.

Option B (Modeling)

Read aloud with students the lesson title and the Spelling Words. Use this model sentence to introduce the lesson skill in a context.

*I will **respect** the decision about my **manuscript**.*

Teaching the Lesson

- Have students name Spelling Words that include the meaning "to write." List the words on the board under the heading *inscribe* (meaning "to write on something"). *(scribe, script, descriptive, description, prescribed, scribbled, inscription, subscription, transcripts)*
- Follow the same procedure for the words that include the meaning "to look at" or "to see." *(inspect, suspect, inspector, spectacle, spectacular, spectrum, spectators)*
- After students have added words from their own reading or writing to the columns, call on volunteers to read aloud all the words and underline the roots.

IN SUMMARY Encourage students to summarize the lesson in their own words. Elicit from students that *-scrib-/-script-*, meaning "to write," and *-spect-*, meaning "to look at," are Latin roots found in many words and that their spellings seldom change.

ASSIGNMENT Students can complete the first page of the lesson as a follow-up to the group activity, either in class or as homework.

Lesson 32: Roots *-scrib-/-script-*, *-spect-* *(continued)*

Practicing the Lesson

Spelling Clues: Comparing Spellings

Remind students that one way to check for correct spelling is to write a word several ways and see which looks right. If they still aren't sure, they should look up the word in a dictionary or use the spell-check program on their computers. Tell students that in these Spelling Words the Latin roots are spelled the same way every time they appear. Tell them to begin their proofreading by looking at the Latin roots of the words. APPLYING SPELLING STRATEGIES

Transitional Spellers Tell students that in this week's Spelling Words the Latin roots are spelled the same way every time they appear. Have students add the roots and their meanings to their Spelling Logs. Then have them write the words on the left-hand side of a study sheet with a plus sign between the root and component parts. In the middle of the page, have them write an "equals" sign (=). To the right of the sign, have them rewrite the word, joining the parts. All words that contain the same root should be written together. Here's an example: pre + scrib + ed = prescribed. VISUALIZING

Proofreading

You may wish to have students review Spelling Clues: Comparing Spellings before proofreading the travel hints.

Fun with Words

You may want to extend the activity by having students create descriptions for the other Spelling Words and then trade papers to see whether their classmates can identify the Spelling Words that belong with the descriptions.

Posttest

Administer the test on page 72 as a posttest, or administer one of your own. Say each word, use it in a sentence, and then repeat the word.

Reteaching the Lesson

Have students write the words still causing them trouble on 3 × 5 cards. Check for correct spelling. Write the Latin roots *-scrib-/-script-* and *-spect-* on the board, and tell students to trace over those letters aloud as they do. Then, one word at a time, have them close their eyes and imagine the root in the word. Finally, have them turn the card over, spell the word on paper, and then check for accuracy. VISUAL/KINESTHETIC MODALITIES

(Pretest/Posttest, continued)

13. I took out a **subscription** to *Cricket* magazine.
14. The visual **spectrum** includes all the colors the average person can see.
15. Do you expect many **spectators** at the parade?
16. We need **transcripts** from all the schools you've attended.

PRACTICE ACTIVITY

The practice activity is on page 169.

Answers: Spelling Clues

1. scribbled
2. suspect
3. inspector
4. subscription
5. transcripts
6. description

Answers: Proofreading

7. descriptive
8. inscription
9. spectacular
10. spectators
11. prescribed
12. inspect

Answers: Fun with Words

13. scribe
14. script
15. spectacle
16. spectrum

Lesson 33: Roots *-rupt-*, *-ject-*

OBJECTIVE

To spell words with the Latin roots *-rupt-* and *-ject-*

HOME ACTIVITY

The home activity is on page 171.

SECOND-LANGUAGE SUPPORT

Students learning English may have an advantage in spelling some of these words because they tend to pronounce each letter of a word. Write on the board the Spelling Words that end in *t*. Pronounce them one at a time, stressing the sound of the final *t*. Have students repeat the words after you. Then call upon volunteers to come to the board and spell the words aloud as they point to each letter. MAKING SOUND-LETTER CORRESPONDENCES

PRETEST/POSTTEST

1. The customers **objected** to the rising prices.
2. We **projected** a gain of $500 for the league from our kick-a-thon.
3. If anyone has any **objections,** please let us know tonight.
4. The **projections** of weather forecasters are for a mild winter.
5. Do you think the volcano will **erupt**?
6. Why was his departure so **abrupt**?
7. She was **bankrupt,** so she couldn't make her house payments.
8. I was trying to **inject** a little humor into a dull conversation.
9. That noise is **disrupting** our study time.
10. Imagine the **disruption** that four St. Bernard puppies would cause!
11. The escape pod will **eject** from the ship automatically in an emergency.

(continued on next page)

Pretest

Administer the test on this page as a pretest. Say each word, use it in the sentence, and then repeat the word. ACCESSING PRIOR KNOWLEDGE

SELF-CHECK Have students check their own pretests against the list of Spelling Words. Remind students to write misspelled words in their Lesson Word Logs. STUDENT SELF-ASSESSMENT

Introducing the Lesson

Option A (Open Sort)

Distribute the word cards (page 170) to individuals or small groups, and guide them in an open-sort activity. In open sort, students group the word cards according to a criterion they select themselves. Then, guide students in comparing and discussing the criteria they selected.

Option B (Modeling)

Read aloud with students the lesson title and the Spelling Words. Use this model sentence to introduce the lesson skill in a context.

*Her science **project** is about the **eruption** of a volcano.*

Teaching the Lesson

- Ask students to name the Latin root that means "to break." Have volunteers name Spelling Words that include the meaning "to break." List the words on the board under the heading *-rupt-*. *(erupt, abrupt, bankrupt, disrupting, disruption, rupture, corrupt, interrupt)*
- Follow the same procedure for the words that include the meaning "to throw." *(objected, projected, objections, projections, inject, eject, reject, rejected)*
- Encourage students to look for other words with these Latin roots and have them add the words to the columns. Call upon volunteers to read the words aloud and underline the roots.

IN SUMMARY Encourage students to summarize the lesson in their own words. Elicit from students the information that *-rupt-*, meaning "to break," and *-ject-*, meaning "to throw," are Latin roots found in many words and that their spellings seldom change.

ASSIGNMENT Students can complete the first page of the lesson as a follow-up to the group activity, either in class or as homework.

Lesson 33: Roots *-rupt-*, *-ject-* *(continued)*

Practicing the Lesson

Spelling Clues: Roots

Tell students first to look at the Latin roots of the words and then to listen for the other sounds of the word and think of the combinations of letters that normally spell the sounds. Tell them to think about prefixes (like *dis-* and *pro-*) and word endings (like *-ed*) and how they are spelled, too. Then have students complete the activity individually or with a partner. APPLYING SPELLING STRATEGIES

TRANSITIONAL SPELLERS To help students recognize the roots, have them write the words with plus signs between the root and other component parts on the left-hand side of a sheet of paper. In the middle of the page, have them write an equals sign (=). To the right of the sign, have them write the word, joining the parts. For example: e + rupt = erupt, dis + rupt + ion = disruption, pro + ject + ed = projected.

Suggest to students that they write first all the words with the root *-rupt-* and then all the words with the root *-ject-*. VISUALIZING

Proofreading

You may wish to have students review Spelling Clues: Roots before proofreading the paragraph.

Fun with Words

Have students complete the captions with words they did not use in lines 1–13. Remind them that the pictures can help them identify the word.

Posttest

Administer the test on page 74 as a posttest, or administer one of your own. Say each word, use it in a sentence, and then repeat the word.

Reteaching the Lesson

Provide students with magnetic letters or cut-out letters with an adhesive on the back. (You will need two alphabet sets per student.) Give each student two magnetic strips or papers backed by adhesive, one with the Latin root *-rupt-* printed on it and one with the Latin root *-ject-*. (The letters in the roots should be the same size as the alphabet sets of letters.) Have students look at the spelling list and use the letters and roots to spell the Spelling Words, one at a time. KINESTHETIC MODALITY

(Pretest/Posttest, continued)

12. Mr. Walsh will **reject** your paper if there are more than five spelling errors.
13. When the squad didn't choose Amy, I felt I would also be **rejected.**
14. Sharp stones will cause these tires to **rupture.**
15. The **corrupt** contractor tried to bribe the inspector.
16. We **interrupt** this broadcast for an important announcement.

PRACTICE ACTIVITY

The practice activity is on page 172.

Answers: Spelling Clues

1. disruption
2. eject
3. erupt
4. objected
5. projected
6. rupture
7. objections
8. bankrupt

Answers: Proofreading

9. interrupt
10. inject
11. reject
12. disrupting
13. abrupt

Answers: Fun with Words

14. rejected
15. corrupt
16. projections

Unit 6 Review

OBJECTIVES

- To review spelling patterns and strategies in Lessons 30–33
- To give students the opportunity to recognize and use these spelling patterns and Spelling Words in their writing

UNIT 6 WORDS

The following words are reviewed in Practice Test, Parts A and B.

Lesson 30: Suffixes in Combination

carefully ownership
actively joyfully

Lesson 31: Prefix *in- (im-, il-, ir-)*

illegal impolite
indefinite informal
independent impure

Lesson 32: Roots *-scrib-/-script-, -spect-*

spectacular inspect
subscription suspect
script scribe

Lesson 33: Roots *-rupt-, -ject-*

projected reject
corrupt interrupt

Review Strategies

Review with students the following spelling-clue strategies for Lessons 30–33.

Lesson 30 Spelling Clues: Suffixes

Write the word *beauty* on the board. Ask a volunteer to write the word *beautiful* next to it. Then have students describe how the base word changed to *i* when the suffix *-ful* was added. Remind students that sometimes the spelling of a base word changes when a suffix is added.

Lesson 31 Spelling Clues: Visual Clues

Have students close their eyes. Then, say the word *independent* aloud. Ask students to picture the word in their minds and then to write the word on paper. Let volunteers put their responses on the board (*independant* or *independent*, for example). After students identify the correct spelling, point out that remembering how a word looks before writing it can help in spelling the word.

Lesson 32 Spelling Clues: Comparing Spellings

Say the word *spectacular*. Have some students write on the board possible spellings for the word. Compare the spellings (*spectaculer*, *specktacular*, and *spectacular*, for example). Ask students which spelling is correct. Remind students that when they are unsure of a word's spelling, they can write the word several different ways and then choose the spelling that looks correct.

Lesson 33 Spelling Clues: Roots

Write the words *disruption* and *erupt* on the board. Ask students what root both words have in common (*-rupt-*). Follow the same procedure with the words *reject* and *projected*. Have students identify the root *-ject-*. Emphasize that knowing how to spell a Latin root can help them spell an entire word that contains the root.

Unit 6 Review *(continued)*

Practice Test

The Practice Test provides an opportunity to review Spelling Words and spelling generalizations in a standardized test format, complete with a sample answer card.

Option 1

Use Practice Test: Part A as a pretest. Later, use Practice Test: Part B as a posttest.

Option 2

Have students review their Lesson Word Log for this unit. If they need extra help, you may wish to review the spelling generalizations discussed in the individual lessons. Then administer both parts of the Practice Test to determine whether students have mastered the spelling generalizations.

Practice Test: Part A	Practice Test: Part B
1. (B) carefully	1. (B) script
2. (D) actively	2. (A) inspect
3. (C) ownership	3. (D) impolite
4. (A) illegal	4. (C) informal
5. (C) indefinite	5. (C) reject
6. (B) independent	6. (B) suspect
7. (C) spectacular	7. (D) joyfully
8. (B) subscription	8. (D) interrupt
9. (A) projected	9. (B) scribe
10. (D) corrupt	10. (C) impure

Options for Evaluation

- Have students check their own Practice Tests against their lists of Spelling Words. The list on the opposite page provides references to the lessons where they can find words they misspelled.
- You may prefer to assign partners and have students check each other's Practice Tests, using their own list of Spelling Words.

REVIEW ACTIVITIES

Activity 1

Have students choose a word from this review lesson and find one or more smaller words within the word. For example, the word *independent* includes the words *in, depend, pen, pend, end, den,* and *dent.* Have students say the small words to a partner, who may then try to guess the large word.

Activity 2

For students who need reteaching, read aloud or write on the board the generalization from one of the lessons in the unit. Then challenge students to identify the words in this lesson that match each generalization. Have students spell each word aloud as they identify it.

Activity 3

Have students choose a word from this review lesson to look up in a dictionary. Then have them create clues based on the information they find in the entry. For example: "This word comes from the Latin root meaning 'write.' It may be used as a noun or as a verb. It can refer to the copy of a play or to handwriting. What is the word?" *(script)* Have other students listen carefully to the clues and then guess the word. A student who guesses the word correctly should then spell it aloud.

Activity 4

Challenge students to create a conversation or short scene in which the dialogue incorporates many of the words from this lesson. Invite students to act out their conversations or scenes with classmates. Let other students listen carefully and identify spelling words as they hear them. Have them spell each word aloud when they recognize it in the dialogue.

Unit 6 Review *(continued)*

WHAT'S IN A WORD?

bankrupt

Another way of saying that a person is short of money is to say that the person is "broke." You might use this opportunity to introduce the concept of *formal speech, colloquial* (informal) *speech,* and *slang* (substandard or trendy speech). You may want to look up the word *broke* in two or three different dictionaries and see if it is identified as a colloquial word that shouldn't be used in formal writing.

WORKING TOGETHER Students might enjoy working with a thesaurus in small groups to find how many ways there are to express the concepts of poverty and wealth. They might begin by looking up *bankrupt* or *penniless* and *fortune* or *affluent.*

♦ ***cordially***

Some etymologists believe that the word *core* comes from the Latin *cor.* Ask students why they agree or disagree with the idea that core comes from *cor.*

SECOND-LANGUAGE SUPPORT Students who speak Latin-based languages may be able to share words that contain the Latin root *-cor-.*

♦ ***incredible***

Have students list synonyms for the word *incredible.* Then have them use in sentences the words they have listed.

SECOND-LANGUAGE SUPPORT Students who speak Latin-based languages may be able to share words from their language that contain the Latin root *credere.* Examples may include *creer* (Spanish for "to believe") and *incroyable* (French for "unbelievable").

♦ This indicates a Unit Spelling Word.

Unit Activity Options

Challenge Yourself

You may want to extend the activity by having students number the blanks and write the missing words on a separate sheet of paper. Then they can trade papers with a classmate and review additional Spelling Words.

Pick a Card, Any Card

You may want to add words with Latin roots to the deck of cards.

Camping Partners

To help students develop ideas for their paragraphs, you may want to display photos or drawings of several items related to camping—tents, canteens, fishing equipment, and so on. Then have students work independently to write their own paragraphs before exchanging paragraphs with a partner.

WORKING TOGETHER You may want to pair students of different levels of spelling proficiency for the paragraph completion activity.

Team Charades

Ask volunteers to demonstrate one or two of the clues before actually beginning the activity.

WORKING TOGETHER Some students might enjoy charades more if they play with a partner. You may want to have students form groups of eight and have members of each group form four teams. The partners on each team can work together to act out the clues.

Proofreading Partners

Encourage partners to discuss their ideas for paragraphs. Remind them that, to include the listed words, they may need to create an unusual or even a fantastic situation in their paragraphs.

Your Word Histories

Encourage partners to look up the words they have entered in their Lesson Word Logs to learn more about their etymologies. Make sure that the dictionaries students will be using in this activity include etymological information.

A Final Scramble

You may want to extend the activity by selecting one scrambled form of each Spelling Word and giving copies of the list to all students for unscrambling.

Unit 6 Review *(continued)*

Curriculum Options

Science: Technically Speaking

This game is played like "Password," with four students, two on each team. A fifth student is the host. Select a visual learner as the host. The host has fifteen or twenty cards; a technical or scientific word with a Greek or Latin root is written on each card. (Include the Spelling Words *inspector, description, prescribed,* and *spectrum.*) The host gives a card to one of the players on Team A. That player defines the word for his or her teammate without using the word itself.

If the teammate guesses the word and spells it correctly, Team A gets a point. If the player guesses wrong, a player from Team B gives his or her teammate a different clue for the same word. If the teammate guesses the word and spells it correctly, Team B gets the point. If not, Team A gets another turn, and so on. Teams take turns starting each new word.

Art: Inspired by Words

Have students choose one word with the Latin root *-ject-* and one word with the Latin root *-rupt-* and write each one, using script, about three inches high, on separate pieces of drawing paper. Using the written word as inspiration, students can turn either word into a piece of art. They might begin both pieces of art to see which they like better. Allow for creativity. When they are finished, post some of the art around the room. See if visitors can find the word in the art piece.

Language Arts: Expanding and Contracting Words

Have each student pick a partner. One student uses a Spelling Word or the base word from which the Spelling Word comes in a sentence, and the partner makes up a sentence using either an expanded or a contracted form of the word.

EXAMPLE:

Student 1: That was an *illegal* chess move.

Student 2: Is sixteen the *legal* driving age?

Then students reverse roles.

Student 2: The colonies received their *independence* from England.

Student 1: Can I *depend* on you?

Students get one point for every word they can expand or contract, provided that the new word is spelled correctly. Play continues until students have used all their Spelling Words or base words in sentences.

WHAT'S IN A WORD?

♦ *inexpensive* and *cheap*

Extend the activity by having students work together to write sentences expressing the different levels of meaning between the two words *inexpensive* and *cheap.*

peace

Extend the activity by having students list stories that communicate the theme of peace whether or not the word *peace* is used in the title.

♦ This indicates a Unit Spelling Word.

Management Charts

This section of the Teacher's Guide contains the following reproducible management charts.

Percent Conversion Chart

The Percent Conversion Chart indicates percentage scores for tests that have from 4 to 24 test items. To find the percentage score a particular student has earned, find the box where the appropriate horizontal and vertical rows meet. The percent score appears in that box.

Spelling Progress Chart

The Spelling Progress Chart may be used to track individual students' scores for the Pretest, Posttest, and the Practice Test over the course of six units. Make one photocopy of the Spelling Progress Chart for each student. Keep a copy of the Spelling Progress Chart for each student. Keep a copy of this chart in each student's portfolio and refer to it during student-and-teacher conferences. If you prefer, you may want to allow the students themselves to record and to keep a copy of the record to monitor their own progress as a form of self-assessment.

The Practice Test at the end of each unit is designed to give students practice with the standardized test format and help them become comfortable with test-taking procedures. The number of correctly spelled words should be recorded in the appropriate column of the chart.

Class Record-Keeping Chart

Use the Class Record-Keeping Chart to keep track of the progress of your class. This chart can hold all students' scores for the Pretest, the Posttest, and the Practice Test. Make six copies of this page. Use one copy with each unit.

Error Analysis Chart for Writing Activities

The Error Analysis Chart for Writing Activities is designed to help you analyze the nature of students' spelling errors and thereby customize instruction to meet individual needs.

Percent Conversion Chart

Use the matrix below to convert the raw score for each test to a percentage.

Number of Test Items ▼ / Number Correct ▶	2	3	4	5	6	7	8	9	10	11	12	13	14	15	16	17	18	19	20	21	22	23	24
For 4-item test	50	75	100																				
For 5-item test	40	60	80	100																			
For 6-item test		50	67	83	100																		
For 7-item test		43	57	71	86	100																	
For 8-item test			50	63	75	88	100																
For 9-item test			44	56	67	78	89	100															
For 10-item test				50	60	70	80	90	100														
For 11-item test				45	55	64	73	82	91	100													
For 12-item test					50	58	67	75	83	92	100												
For 13-item test					46	54	62	69	77	85	92	100											
For 14-item test						50	57	64	71	79	86	93	100										
For 15-item test						47	53	60	67	73	80	87	93	100									
For 16-item test							50	56	63	69	75	81	88	94	100								
For 17-item test							47	53	59	65	71	76	82	88	94	100							
For 18-item test								50	56	61	67	72	78	83	89	94	100						
For 19-item test								47	53	58	63	68	74	79	84	89	95	100					
For 20-item test									50	55	60	65	70	75	80	85	90	95	100				
For 21-item test									48	52	57	62	67	71	76	81	86	90	95	100			
For 22-item test										50	55	59	64	68	73	77	82	86	91	95	100		
For 23-item test										48	52	57	61	65	70	74	78	83	87	91	96	100	
For 24-item test											50	54	58	63	67	71	75	79	83	88	92	96	100

NAME ______________________ CLASS ______________ DATE ______________

Spelling Progress Chart

Directions Write in Pretest, Posttest, and Practice Test scores. If a student shows improvement but has missed one or more items, fill in dot under Showed Improvement. For perfect scores, fill in dot under Mastered Words.

		NUMBER OF WORDS CORRECTLY SPELLED		PROGRESS	
LESSON		Pretest	Posttest	Showed Improvement	Mastered Words
Unit 1	Lesson 1			○	○
	Lesson 2			○	○
	Lesson 3			○	○
	Lesson 4			○	○
	Unit 1 Review Practice Test			○	○
	Lesson 6			○	○
Unit 2	Lesson 7			○	○
	Lesson 8			○	○
	Lesson 9			○	○
	Lesson 10			○	○
	Unit 2 Review Practice Test			○	○
	Lesson 12			○	○
Unit 3	Lesson 13			○	○
	Lesson 14			○	○
	Lesson 15			○	○
	Lesson 16			○	○
	Unit 3 Review Practice Test			○	○
	Lesson 18			○	○
Unit 4	Lesson 19			○	○
	Lesson 20			○	○
	Lesson 21			○	○
	Lesson 22			○	○
	Unit 4 Review Practice Test			○	○
	Lesson 24			○	○
Unit 5	Lesson 25			○	○
	Lesson 26			○	○
	Lesson 27			○	○
	Lesson 28			○	○
	Unit 5 Review Practice Test			○	○
	Lesson 30			○	○
Unit 6	Lesson 31			○	○
	Lesson 32			○	○
	Lesson 33			○	○
	Unit 6 Review Practice Test			○	○

Class Record-Keeping Chart

Directions Make six copies of this page, and use one copy with each unit.

	LESSON	LESSON	LESSON	LESSON	LESSON	UNIT REVIEW
NAME	Pretest/ Posttest	Pretest/ Posttest	Pretest/ Posttest	Pretest/ Posttest	Pretest/ Posttest	Practice Test

NAME ______________________ CLASS ______________ DATE ______________

Error Analysis Chart for Writing Activities

Directions Make as many copies of this chart as necessary.

		Where the Error Appears in the Word			Substitutions, Omissions, Insertions, Reversals				Other		
Misspelling	Correct Spelling	Beginning	Middle	End	Vowel	Consonant	Silent Letters	Double Letters	Compounds, Homophones, Contractions	Irregular Words	Inflectional Endings and Suffixes

Student Worksheets and Answer Key

This section of the Teacher's Guide contains the following reproducible worksheets and answers.

Word Cards
The Word Cards are designed to be used in open-sort activities. In open sort, students group the word cards according to a criterion they select themselves. They might group words that share the same beginning or middle sound, words that are related by topic, or words that have a similar shape.

Home Activities
The Home Activity is designed to involve family members in the spelling instruction of your students. It includes a brief introductory letter about the lesson being developed in class as well as an activity designed to help family members become an integral part of the learning process.

Practice Activities
The Practice Activity is designed to provide students with additional practice on the spelling concepts developed in class.

Answer Key for Practice Activities
The Answer Key for Practice Activities provides answers for all Practice Activities.

NAME ______ CLASS ______ DATE ______

Lesson 1: Short Vowels

WORD CARDS

sack	admit	rapid	glance
contact	contract	advance	depth
comment	summit	sketch	nonsense
splendid	ethnic	liquid	impulse

Lesson 1: Short Vowels

HOME ACTIVITY

Dear Parent or Guardian,

Your child ______________________ has just begun this spelling lesson. This week's test of words will be held on

____________________________________ .

Please contact me if you have any questions. Use the Comment Box to make any comments on your child's progress, noting any words that he or she still needs to review.

Sincerely,

____

Spelling Words

1. sack
2. admit
3. rapid
4. glance
5. contact
6. contract
7. advance
8. depth
9. comment
10. summit
11. sketch
12. nonsense
13. splendid
14. ethnic
15. liquid
16. impulse

Home Activity

Have your child prepare a word search. Draw a 9 × 9 grid of cells. Ask your child to write the Spelling Words horizontally or vertically in the grid. Fill the remaining cells with random letters. Then have a family member find the Spelling Words.

COMMENT BOX

NAME ______________________ CLASS ______________ DATE ______________

Lesson 1: Short Vowels

PRACTICE ACTIVITY

A. Complete the crossword puzzle with Spelling Words.

Across
1. wonderful
5. touch
7. fast
9. bag
10. urge
11. peak
12. deepness
14. peek
15. agreement

Down
1. drawing
2. foolishness
3. remark
4. a drink
6. move ahead
8. confess
13. kind of background

B. Write a paragraph on a topic of your choice. Use at least five Spelling Words.

Spelling Words

1. sack
2. admit
3. rapid
4. glance
5. contact
6. contract
7. advance
8. depth
9. comment
10. summit
11. sketch
12. nonsense
13. splendid
14. ethnic
15. liquid
16. impulse

NAME ______ CLASS ______ DATE ______

Lesson 2: Long Vowels

WORD CARDS

bait	peach	bride	prime
globe	grove	slope	slice
roast	spike	stroke	praise
squeeze	breathe	gross	thigh

Lesson 2: Long Vowels

Dear Parent or Guardian,

Your child ______________________ has just begun this spelling lesson. This week's test of words will be held on ______________________.

Please contact me if you have any questions. Use the Comment Box to make any comments on your child's progress, noting any words that he or she still needs to review.

Sincerely,

____

Spelling Words

1. bait
2. peach
3. bride
4. prime
5. globe
6. grove
7. slope
8. slice
9. roast
10. spike
11. stroke
12. praise
13. squeeze
14. breathe
15. gross
16. thigh

Home Activity

Copy the list of Spelling Words, scrambling the letters in each word. Give the list to your child and ask him or her to unscramble the letters in each word so that the Spelling Words are spelled correctly.

COMMENT BOX

NAME ______________________ CLASS ______________ DATE ______________

Lesson 2: Long Vowels

PRACTICE ACTIVITY

A. Write the Spelling Word that rhymes with each word below.

nice ______________

freeze ______________

high ______________

reach ______________

wait ______________

time ______________

coast ______________

raise ______________

wide ______________

sheathe ______________

robe ______________

hope ______________

Change one vowel in each of these words to spell a Spelling Word.

grave ______________ strike ______________

grass ______________ spoke ______________

B. Write a paragraph on a topic of your choice. Use at least five Spelling Words.

____

____

____

____

____

____

____

____

____

____

____

Spelling Words

1. *bait*
2. *peach*
3. *bride*
4. *prime*
5. *globe*
6. *grove*
7. *slope*
8. *slice*
9. *roast*
10. *spike*
11. *stroke*
12. *praise*
13. *squeeze*
14. *breathe*
15. *gross*
16. *thigh*

NAME ______ CLASS ______ DATE ______

Lesson 3: Variant Vowels

WORD CARDS

count	county	salt	cross
shout	youth	amount	pounds
mountain	thousands	proof	crawled
account	launched	rumors	saucer

Lesson 3: Variant Vowels

HOME ACTIVITY

Dear Parent or Guardian,

Your child ______________________ has just begun this spelling lesson. This week's test of words will be held on

______________________________________ .

Please contact me if you have any questions. Use the Comment Box to make any comments on your child's progress, noting any words that he or she still needs to review.

Sincerely,

____

Spelling Words

1. count
2. county
3. salt
4. cross
5. shout
6. youth
7. amount
8. pounds
9. mountain
10. thousands
11. proof
12. crawled
13. account
14. launched
15. rumors
16. saucer

Home Activity

Prepare a list using the Spelling Words. Beginning with the second letter of each word, substitute a dash for every other letter. Give the list to your child, and ask him or her to finish spelling the words by filling in the blanks.

COMMENT BOX

NAME ______ CLASS ______ DATE ______

Lesson 3: Variant Vowels

PRACTICE ACTIVITY

A. Add and subtract the letters as shown. Write each Spelling Word.

prove – ve + of = ______
laundry – dry + ched = ______
crop – p + ss = ______
sausage – sage + cer = ______
couch – ch + nt = ______
crash – sh + wled = ______
pour – r + nds = ______
sale – e + t = ______
accordion – rdion + unt = ______
young – ng + th = ______
course – rse + nty = ______
thought – ght + sands = ______
rumble – ble + ors = ______
mouse – se + ntain = ______
among – ng + unt = ______
shove – ve + ut = ______

B. Write a paragraph on a topic of your choice. Use at least five Spelling Words.

______
______
______
______
______
______
______
______
______
______
______
______
______

Spelling Words

1. count
2. county
3. salt
4. cross
5. shout
6. youth
7. amount
8. pounds
9. mountain
10. thousands
11. proof
12. crawled
13. account
14. launched
15. rumors
16. saucer

NAME ______ CLASS ______ DATE ______

Lesson 4: Vowels Before *r*

WORD CARDS

roar	apart	reward	worse
turtle	nightmare	burnt	curb
purse	declare	scarce	inserts
sparkling	source	nervous	warrant

Lesson 4: Vowels Before *r*

Dear Parent or Guardian,

Your child ______________________ has just begun this spelling lesson. This week's test of words will be held on ______________________.

Please contact me if you have any questions. Use the Comment Box to make any comments on your child's progress, noting any words that he or she still needs to review.

Sincerely,

____

Spelling Words

1. roar
2. apart
3. reward
4. worse
5. turtle
6. nightmare
7. burnt
8. curb
9. purse
10. declare
11. scarce
12. inserts
13. sparkling
14. source
15. nervous
16. warrant

Home Activity

Prepare a simple definition for each Spelling Word. Read the definition, and ask your child to write the Spelling Word that corresponds to the definition.

COMMENT BOX

NAME CLASS DATE

Lesson 4: Vowels Before *r*

PRACTICE ACTIVITY

A. Read the consonants for each Spelling Word. Think of the vowel or vowels that are missing. Write the word.

scrc ____________

rwrd ____________

wrrnt ____________

brnt ____________

rr ____________

prs ____________

nrvs ____________

nghtmr ____________

prt ____________

nsrts ____________

crb ____________

src ____________

dclr ____________

wrs ____________

trtl ____________

sprklng ____________

B. Write a paragraph on a topic of your choice. Use at least five Spelling Words.

Spelling Words

1. roar
2. apart
3. reward
4. worse
5. turtle
6. nightmare
7. burnt
8. curb
9. purse
10. declare
11. scarce
12. inserts
13. sparkling
14. source
15. nervous
16. warrant

NAME CLASS DATE

Lesson 6: Other Vowel Spellings

WORD CARDS

busy	among	building	young
enough	though	straight	rough
courage	eighth	system	although
sleigh	boulder	biscuit	dough

Lesson 6: Other Vowel Spellings

Dear Parent or Guardian,

Your child ______________________ has just begun this spelling lesson. This week's test of words will be held on ______________________________ .

Please contact me if you have any questions. Use the Comment Box to make any comments on your child's progress, noting any words that he or she still needs to review.

Sincerely,

____

Spelling Words

1. busy
2. among
3. building
4. young
5. enough
6. though
7. straight
8. rough
9. courage
10. eighth
11. system
12. although
13. sleigh
14. boulder
15. biscuit
16. dough

Home Activity

Think of a question for each Spelling Word. For example, you might ask, "How would you describe someone who has too much to do?" *(busy)* Have your child say and spell the correct Spelling Word.

COMMENT BOX

NAME ______________________ CLASS ______________ DATE ______________

Lesson 6: Other Vowel Spellings

PRACTICE ACTIVITY

A. Write Spelling Words that sound the same as these words.

strait ______________

bolder ______________

doe ______________

slay ______________

ruff ______________

Add vowels to the groups of letters to make Spelling Words. Write the Spelling Words on the lines. (Hint: Remember that *y* can sometimes be used as a vowel.)

yng ______________

bsct ______________

thgh ______________

bs ______________

bldng ______________

mng ______________

ghth ______________

sstm ______________

lthgh ______________

ngh ______________

crg ______________

B. Write a paragraph on a topic of your choice. Use at least five Spelling Words.

____

____

____

____

____

____

____

____

____

____

Spelling Words

1. busy
2. among
3. building
4. young
5. enough
6. though
7. straight
8. rough
9. courage
10. eighth
11. system
12. although
13. sleigh
14. boulder
15. biscuit
16. dough

NAME CLASS DATE

Lesson 7: Words with *ie* and *ei*

WORD CARDS

boyfriend	girlfriend	mischief	pier
freight	foreign	receive	receiver
belief	relief	weighed	reins
fierce	heights	thieves	achieve

Lesson 7: Words with *ie* and *ei*

Dear Parent or Guardian,

Your child ____________________ has just begun this spelling lesson. This week's test of words will be held on ____________________.

Please contact me if you have any questions. Use the Comment Box to make any comments on your child's progress, noting any words that he or she still needs to review.

Sincerely,

____

Spelling Words

1. boyfriend
2. girlfriend
3. mischief
4. pier
5. freight
6. foreign
7. receive
8. receiver
9. belief
10. relief
11. weighed
12. reins
13. fierce
14. heights
15. thieves
16. achieve

Home Activity

Copy the list of Spelling Words, scrambling the letters in each word. Give the list to your child, and ask him or her to unscramble the letters in each word so that the Spelling Words are spelled correctly.

COMMENT BOX

NAME ______________________ CLASS ______________ DATE ______________

Lesson 7: Words with *ie* and *ei*

PRACTICE ACTIVITY

A. Write the Spelling Words that complete the crossword puzzle.

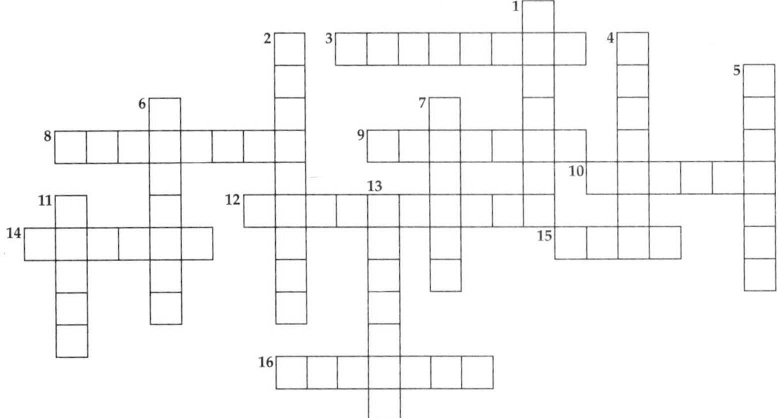

Across

3. one who catches the football
8. troublemaking
9. cargo
10. savage
12. a female friend
14. trust; confidence
15. ship's landing place
16. peaks

Down

1. measured
2. a male friend
4. to accept
5. robbers
6. to reach by effort
7. a freeing from pain or hardship
11. straps for guiding horses
13. from another country

B. Write a paragraph on a topic of your choice. Use at least five Spelling Words.

____

____

____

____

____

____

____

____

____

____

____

____

Spelling Words

1. boyfriend
2. girlfriend
3. mischief
4. pier
5. freight
6. foreign
7. receive
8. receiver
9. belief
10. relief
11. weighed
12. reins
13. fierce
14. heights
15. thieves
16. achieve

NAME CLASS DATE

Lesson 8: Compound Words

WORD CARDS

greenhouse	seashore	fireworks	fun-loving
New Year	fairy tales	bedtime	cupboard
upright	teenager	thunderstorm	barefoot
mean-spirited	middle-aged	bodyguard	so-called

Lesson 8: Compound Words

HOME ACTIVITY

Dear Parent or Guardian,

Your child ______________________ has just begun this spelling lesson. This week's test of words will be held on

______________________________________ .

Please contact me if you have any questions. Use the Comment Box to make any comments on your child's progress, noting any words that he or she still needs to review.

Sincerely,

____

Spelling Words

1. greenhouse
2. seashore
3. fireworks
4. fun-loving
5. New Year
6. fairy tales
7. bedtime
8. cupboard
9. upright
10. teenager
11. thunderstorm
12. barefoot
13. mean-spirited
14. middle-aged
15. bodyguard
16. so-called

Home Activity

Prepare a flashcard for each Spelling Word. Show your child each card for a few seconds, and then place it facedown on the table. Ask your child to spell the word you just showed him or her.

COMMENT BOX

NAME ______________________ CLASS ______________ DATE ______________

Lesson 8: Compound Words

PRACTICE ACTIVITY

A. Use the words in the boxes to help you write Spelling Words for each category. Write the compound Spelling Words on the lines.

1. Ways to be

fun foot mean up

______________ ______________

______________ ______________

____

2. Exciting things

fire shore tales storm

______________ ______________

______________ ______________

3. Times and places to keep things

bed cup house

______________ ______________

____

4. Kinds of people

guard teen

______________ ______________

5. Time of changes

new

____

6. Supposed

called

____

B. Write a paragraph on a topic of your choice. Use at least five Spelling Words.

____

____

____

____

____

____

Spelling Words

1. greenhouse
2. seashore
3. fireworks
4. fun-loving
5. New Year
6. fairy tales
7. bedtime
8. cupboard
9. upright
10. teenager
11. thunderstorm
12. barefoot
13. mean-spirited
14. middle-aged
15. bodyguard
16. so-called

NAME ______ CLASS ______ DATE ______

Lesson 9: Homophones

WORD CARDS

week	weak	steel	steal
grown	groan	guest	guessed
creek	creak	weather	whether
sore	soar	stake	steak

Lesson 9: Homophones

Dear Parent or Guardian,

Your child ______________________ has just begun this spelling lesson. This week's test of words will be held on ______________________.

Please contact me if you have any questions. Use the Comment Box to make any comments on your child's progress, noting any words that he or she still needs to review.

Sincerely,

____

Spelling Words

1. week
2. weak
3. steel
4. steal
5. grown
6. groan
7. guest
8. guessed
9. creek
10. creak
11. weather
12. whether
13. sore
14. soar
15. stake
16. steak

Home Activity

For each Spelling Word, write a sentence using the word. Read each sentence, leaving out the Spelling Word. Ask your child to write the Spelling Word that best fits the meaning of the sentence.

COMMENT BOX

NAME ______ CLASS ______ DATE ______

Lesson 9: Homophones

PRACTICE ACTIVITY

A. Write the Spelling Word or Words that rhyme with each word *and* that have the same spelling pattern as the word.

meek ______

leak ______

lore ______

flake ______

break ______

heather ______

real ______

tether ______

heel ______

loan ______

roar ______

quest ______

blessed ______

sown ______

B. Write a paragraph on a topic of your choice. Use at least five Spelling Words.

Spelling Words

1. week
2. weak
3. steel
4. steal
5. grown
6. groan
7. quest
8. guessed
9. creek
10. creak
11. weather
12. whether
13. sore
14. soar
15. stake
16. steak

NAME ________________ CLASS ________ DATE ________

Lesson 10: Easily Confused Words

WORD CARDS

later	latter	except	accept
angle	angel	costume	custom
affect	effect	adopt	adapt
device	devise	decent	descent

Lesson 10: Easily Confused Words

Dear Parent or Guardian,

Your child ____________________ has just begun this spelling lesson. This week's test of words will be held on ______________________________.

Please contact me if you have any questions. Use the Comment Box to make any comments on your child's progress, noting any words that he or she still needs to review.

Sincerely,

____

Spelling Words

1. later
2. latter
3. except
4. accept
5. angle
6. angel
7. costume
8. custom
9. affect
10. effect
11. adopt
12. adapt
13. device
14. devise
15. decent
16. descent

Home Activity

For each Spelling Word, ask your child to write a sentence using alliteration. That is, some of the words in the sentence should start with the same sound as that of the Spelling Word. Some of the sentences will probably be tongue twisters!

COMMENT BOX

NAME ______________ CLASS ______________ DATE ______________

Lesson 10: Easily Confused Words

PRACTICE ACTIVITY

A. Make Spelling Words by changing, moving, adding, or subtracting vowels. If the word is already a Spelling Word, form another Spelling Word. Write each Spelling Word.

adapt ______________

effect ______________

angle ______________

costume ______________

liter ______________

letter ______________

devious ______________

Which Spelling Word do you associate with . . .

mathematics? ______________

a play? ______________

an inventor? ______________

a mountain climber? ______________

a good salary? ______________

a gift? ______________

change? ______________

all but one? ______________

the word *cause*? ______________

B. Write a paragraph on a topic of your choice. Use at least five Spelling Words.

____

____

____

____

____

____

____

____

____

Spelling Words

1. later
2. latter
3. except
4. accept
5. angle
6. angel
7. costume
8. custom
9. affect
10. effect
11. adopt
12. adapt
13. device
14. devise
15. decent
16. descent

NAME ________________ CLASS ________________ DATE ________________

Lesson 12: Changing *y* to *i*

WORD CARDS

cities	mummies	supplies	families
varied	centuries	colonies	applies
occupied	identified	enemies	activities
denied	allied	industries	qualified

Lesson 12: Changing *y* to *i*

Dear Parent or Guardian,

Your child ________________________ *has just begun this spelling lesson. This week's test of words will be held on* ________________________.

Please contact me if you have any questions. Use the Comment Box to make any comments on your child's progress, noting any words that he or she still needs to review.

Sincerely,

____

Spelling Words

1. *cities*
2. *mummies*
3. *supplies*
4. *families*
5. *varied*
6. *centuries*
7. *colonies*
8. *applies*
9. *occupied*
10. *identified*
11. *enemies*
12. *activities*
13. *denied*
14. *allied*
15. *industries*
16. *qualified*

Home Activity

Prepare a simple definition for each Spelling Word. Read the definition, and ask your child to write the Spelling Word that corresponds to the definition.

COMMENT BOX

Lesson 12: Changing *y* to *i*

PRACTICE ACTIVITY

A. Circle each Spelling Word hidden in the puzzle. Then write the word on the line.

```
c l (1)i d e n t i f i e d i n g
p r o s h e (2)v a r i e d r o n
a r c h (3)i n d u s t r i e s h
g l a i (4)c o l o n i e s p u r
i t s m e i s h (5)c i t i e s e
d r (6)a c t i v i t i e s p o q
e n o u (7)q u a l i f i e d a x
b r i (8)e n e m i e s h o u l y
p r e s i (9)m u m m i e s o l e
s a r a h s (10)f a m i l i e s t
n u (11)o c c u p i e d u d d l e
p e l l o s (12)c e n t u r i e s
v e s k a (13)d e n i e d a n d a
o s (14)s u p p l i e s t u m p e
s (15)a l l i e d e a x i n i t y
c l e v a j (16)a p p l i e s p y
```

1. ______________ 9. ______________
2. ______________ 10. ______________
3. ______________ 11. ______________
4. ______________ 12. ______________
5. ______________ 13. ______________
6. ______________ 14. ______________
7. ______________ 15. ______________
8. ______________ 16. ______________

Spelling Words

1. cities
2. mummies
3. supplies
4. families
5. varied
6. centuries
7. colonies
8. applies
9. occupied
10. identified
11. enemies
12. activities
13. denied
14. allied
15. industries
16. qualified

B. Write a paragraph on a topic of your choice. Use at least five Spelling Words.

____

____

____

____

NAME _______________ CLASS _______________ DATE _______________

Lesson 13: Endings /ər/, /əl/, /ən/

WORD CARDS

reader	speaker	layer	American
beaten	musical	rotten	German
Indian	Roman	explorer	stretcher
critical	criminal	political	original

Lesson 13: Endings /ər/, /əl/, /ən/

Dear Parent or Guardian,

Your child ______________________ has just begun this spelling lesson. This week's test of words will be held on

______________________________ .

Please contact me if you have any questions. Use the Comment Box to make any comments on your child's progress, noting any words that he or she still needs to review.

Sincerely,

____

Spelling Words

1. reader
2. speaker
3. layer
4. American
5. beaten
6. musical
7. rotten
8. German
9. Indian
10. Roman
11. explorer
12. stretcher
13. critical
14. criminal
15. political
16. original

Home Activity

Ask your child to write an acrostic. Have your child write one of the Spelling Words vertically. For each letter in the Spelling Word, have him or her write a phrase that starts with that letter. Encourage your child to do several acrostics each day.

COMMENT BOX

NAME ______ CLASS ______ DATE ______

Lesson 13: Endings /ər/, /əl/, /ən/

PRACTICE ACTIVITY

A. Write the Spelling Word that is related to each word below.

speech ______
criticize ______
originate ______
Germany ______
lay ______
reading ______
Rome ______
beat ______
politics ______
stretch ______
America ______
musician ______
crime ______
India ______
rot ______
exploration ______

B. Write a paragraph on a topic of your choice. Use at least five Spelling Words.

Spelling Words

1. reader
2. speaker
3. layer
4. American
5. beaten
6. musical
7. rotten
8. German
9. Indian
10. Roman
11. explorer
12. stretcher
13. critical
14. criminal
15. political
16. original

NAME CLASS DATE

Lesson 14: Patterns—VC/CV Words

WORD CARDS

pillow	indeed	monster	fifteen
escape	gotten	velvet	engine
insist	admire	index	intense
further	frantic	convince	instinct

Lesson 14: Patterns—VC/CV Words

Dear Parent or Guardian,

Your child ______________________ has just begun this spelling lesson. This week's test of words will be held on ______________________.

Please contact me if you have any questions. Use the Comment Box to make any comments on your child's progress, noting any words that he or she still needs to review.

Sincerely,

____

Spelling Words

1. pillow
2. indeed
3. monster
4. fifteen
5. escape
6. gotten
7. velvet
8. engine
9. insist
10. admire
11. index
12. intense
13. further
14. frantic
15. convince
16. instinct

Home Activity

Copy the list of Spelling Words, scrambling the letters in each word. Give the list to your child, and ask him or her to unscramble the letters in each word so that the Spelling Words are spelled correctly.

COMMENT BOX

NAME ________________ CLASS ________ DATE ________

Lesson 14: Patterns—VC/CV Words

PRACTICE ACTIVITY

A. Use the letter clue to identify each Spelling Word. Write the word.

g _ _ _ _ _ ______________

_ _ _ _ _ _ _ c ______________

_ _ g _ _ _ ______________

_ u _ _ _ _ _ ______________

v _ _ _ _ _ ______________

_ _ _ _ _ _ _ t ______________

_ _ _ _ x ______________

p _ _ _ _ _ ______________

_ _ s _ _ _ ______________

_ _ _ _ _ d ______________

_ s _ _ _ _ ______________

_ _ _ v _ _ _ _ ______________

i _ _ _ _ _ _ ______________

_ _ f _ _ _ _ ______________

m _ _ _ _ _ _ ______________

_ _ _ _ r _ ______________

B. Write a paragraph on a topic of your choice. Use at least five Spelling Words.

____

____

____

____

____

____

____

____

____

____

____

Spelling Words

1. pillow
2. indeed
3. monster
4. fifteen
5. escape
6. gotten
7. velvet
8. engine
9. insist
10. admire
11. index
12. intense
13. further
14. frantic
15. convince
16. instinct

NAME ______________________ CLASS ______________ DATE ______________

Lesson 15: Patterns—V/CV Words

WORD CARDS

Friday	apron	motive	meter
agent	evil	local	eager
famous	fiber	razor	vital
rival	basis	cheetah	scenic

Lesson 15: Patterns—V/CV Words

HOME ACTIVITY

Dear Parent or Guardian,

Your child ____________________ has just begun this spelling lesson. This week's test of words will be held on ____________________ .

Please contact me if you have any questions. Use the Comment Box to make any comments on your child's progress, noting any words that he or she still needs to review.

Sincerely,

____

Spelling Words

1. Friday
2. apron
3. motive
4. meter
5. agent
6. evil
7. local
8. eager
9. famous
10. fiber
11. razor
12. vital
13. rival
14. basis
15. cheetah
16. scenic

Home Activity

Have your child prepare a word search. Draw a 9 × 9 grid of cells. Ask your child to write the Spelling Words horizontally or vertically in the grid. Fill the remaining cells with random letters. Then have a family member find the Spelling Words.

COMMENT BOX

NAME ______ CLASS ______ DATE ______

Lesson 15: Patterns—V/CV Words

PRACTICE ACTIVITY

A. Rearrange the letters to spell a Spelling Word. Write the word.

agree ______
brief ______
vile ______
onpar ______
issab ______
treem ______
Faridy ______
snicce ______
zarro ______
getan ______
livar ______
callo ______
lavit ______
emovit ______
mufaso ______
hehecat ______

B. Write a paragraph on a topic of your choice. Use at least five Spelling Words.

______
______
______
______
______
______
______
______
______
______
______

Spelling Words

1. Friday
2. apron
3. motive
4. meter
5. agent
6. evil
7. local
8. eager
9. famous
10. fiber
11. razor
12. vital
13. rival
14. basis
15. cheetah
16. scenic

NAME ______________________ CLASS ______________ DATE ______________

Lesson 16: Adding *-ed* and *-ing*

WORD CARDS

lifted	cooling	pointed	returned
speaking	spelling	wondered	bragged
healed	scrubbed	answered	threatened
admitted	committed	referring	preferred

Lesson 16: Adding *-ed* and *-ing*

Dear Parent or Guardian,

Your child ______________________ has just begun this spelling lesson. This week's test of words will be held on ______________________.

Please contact me if you have any questions. Use the Comment Box to make any comments on your child's progress, noting any words that he or she still needs to review.

Sincerely,

____

Spelling Words

1. lifted
2. cooling
3. pointed
4. returned
5. speaking
6. spelling
7. wondered
8. bragged
9. healed
10. scrubbed
11. answered
12. threatened
13. admitted
14. committed
15. referring
16. preferred

Home Activity

For each Spelling Word, write a sentence using the word. Read each sentence, leaving out the Spelling Word. Ask your child to write the Spelling Word that best fits the meaning of the sentence.

COMMENT BOX

NAME ______ CLASS ______ DATE ______

Lesson 16: Adding *-ed* and *-ing*

PRACTICE ACTIVITY

A. Write the Spelling Word that matches each clue.

made threats ______

made healthy ______

replied ______

talking ______

aimed at ______

thought ______

talking about ______

came back ______

boasted ______

liked ______

confessed ______

dedicated ______

washed ______

raised ______

a school subject ______

getting colder ______

B. Write a paragraph on a topic of your choice. Use at least five Spelling Words.

______

______

______

______

______

______

______

______

______

______

______

______

Spelling Words

1. lifted
2. cooling
3. pointed
4. returned
5. speaking
6. spelling
7. wondered
8. bragged
9. healed
10. scrubbed
11. answered
12. threatened
13. admitted
14. committed
15. referring
16. preferred

NAME ______ CLASS ______ DATE ______

Lesson 18: Noun Suffix *-ance*/*-ence*

WORD CARDS

importance	entrance	difference	independence
insurance	conference	ambulance	absence
instance	audience	allowance	intelligence
assurance	appearance	obedience	presence

Lesson 18: Noun Suffix *-ance/-ence*

Dear Parent or Guardian,

Your child ______________________ has just begun this spelling lesson. This week's test of words will be held on

______________________________.

Please contact me if you have any questions. Use the Comment Box to make any comments on your child's progress, noting any words that he or she still needs to review.

Sincerely,

____

Spelling Words

1. importance
2. entrance
3. difference
4. independence
5. insurance
6. conference
7. ambulance
8. absence
9. instance
10. audience
11. allowance
12. intelligence
13. assurance
14. appearance
15. obedience
16. presence

Home Activity

For each Spelling Word, ask your child to write a sentence using alliteration. That is, some of the words in the sentence should start with the same sound as that of the Spelling Word. Some of the sentences will probably be tongue twisters!

COMMENT BOX

NAME ______ CLASS ______ DATE ______

Lesson 18: Noun Suffix *-ance*/*-ence*

PRACTICE ACTIVITY

A. Add or change a suffix in each of these words to form a Spelling Word. Write the Spelling Words on the lines.

enter ______
import ______
obey ______
appear ______
present ______
differ ______
allow ______
confer ______
insure ______
intelligent ______
assure ______
independent ______
instant ______
absent ______
amble ______
audition ______

B. Write a paragraph on a topic of your choice. Use at least five Spelling Words.

______

Spelling Words

1. importance
2. entrance
3. difference
4. independence
5. insurance
6. conference
7. ambulance
8. absence
9. instance
10. audience
11. allowance
12. intelligence
13. assurance
14. appearance
15. obedience
16. presence

NAME ______________________ CLASS ______________ DATE ______________

Lesson 19: Suffixes *-ship, -ment, -ity*

WORD CARDS

statement	friendship	leadership	partnership
activity	ability	argument	personality
electricity	championship	community	majority
responsibility	curiosity	necessity	authority

Lesson 19: Suffixes *-ship, -ment, -ity*

HOME ACTIVITY

Dear Parent or Guardian,

Your child ______________________ has just begun this spelling lesson. This week's test of words will be held on ______________________.

Please contact me if you have any questions. Use the Comment Box to make any comments on your child's progress, noting any words that he or she still needs to review.

Sincerely,

____

Spelling Words

1. statement
2. friendship
3. leadership
4. partnership
5. activity
6. ability
7. argument
8. personality
9. electricity
10. championship
11. community
12. majority
13. responsibility
14. curiosity
15. necessity
16. authority

Home Activity

Prepare a flashcard for each Spelling Word. Show your child each card for a few seconds, and then place it facedown on the table. Ask your child to spell the word you just showed him or her.

COMMENT BOX

NAME ______ CLASS ______ DATE ______

Lesson 19: Suffixes *-ship, -ment, -ity*

PRACTICE ACTIVITY

A. Add or change a suffix in each of these words to form a Spelling Word. Make other spelling changes as needed. Write the Spelling Words on the lines.

champion ______

electric ______

need ______

partner ______

argue ______

curious ______

author ______

state ______

leader ______

major ______

active ______

personal ______

able ______

commune ______

responsible ______

friend ______

B. Write a paragraph on a topic of your choice. Use at least five Spelling Words.

______

______

______

______

______

______

______

______

______

______

______

Spelling Words

1. statement
2. friendship
3. leadership
4. partnership
5. activity
6. ability
7. argument
8. personality
9. electricity
10. championship
11. community
12. majority
13. responsibility
14. curiosity
15. necessity
16. authority

NAME ____________________ CLASS ____________________ DATE ____________________

Lesson 20: Prefix *ad- (ac-, as-, af-, ap-)*

WORD CARDS

appointed	accident	affair	assembly
approach	accuse	applause	affection
accompany	assign	appreciate	accurate
association	apparent	accustomed	assistance

Lesson 20: Prefix *ad-* *(ac-, as-, af-, ap-)*

Dear Parent or Guardian,

Your child ______________________ has just begun this spelling lesson. This week's test of words will be held on ______________________.

Please contact me if you have any questions. Use the Comment Box to make any comments on your child's progress, noting any words that he or she still needs to review.

Sincerely,

____

Spelling Words

1. appointed
2. accident
3. affair
4. assembly
5. approach
6. accuse
7. applause
8. affection
9. accompany
10. assign
11. appreciate
12. accurate
13. association
14. apparent
15. accustomed
16. assistance

Home Activity

Think of a question for each Spelling Word. For example, you might ask, "What does someone ask for when help is needed?" *(assistance)* Have your child say and spell the correct Spelling Word.

COMMENT BOX

NAME ____________________ CLASS ____________ DATE ____________

Lesson 20: Prefix *ad-* (*ac-*, *as-*, *af-*, *ap-*)

PRACTICE ACTIVITY

A. Complete the crossword puzzle with Spelling Words.

Across

4. what you feel for a pet
5. to charge with wrongdoing
6. evident, obvious
9. to draw near
12. a school gathering
13. in the habit of
14. a thing not done on purpose
15. to give as a task
16. help or aid

Down

1. selected and given a duty
2. exactly right, correct
3. a social get-together
7. clapping after a performance
8. an organized group
10. to go with, escort
11. to value or enjoy

B. Write a paragraph on a topic of your choice. Use at least five Spelling Words.

____

____

____

____

____

____

____

____

____

Spelling Words

1. *appointed*
2. *accident*
3. *affair*
4. *assembly*
5. *approach*
6. *accuse*
7. *applause*
8. *affection*
9. *accompany*
10. *assign*
11. *appreciate*
12. *accurate*
13. *association*
14. *apparent*
15. *accustomed*
16. *assistance*

NAME ______ CLASS ______ DATE ______

Lesson 21: Prefix *com- (con-)*

WORD CARDS

conviction	commanded	commonly	considered
continued	commander	commit	constitution
confusing	commence	commotion	commercial
communicate	communities	communication	committee

Lesson 21: Prefix *com- (con-)*

HOME ACTIVITY

Dear Parent or Guardian,

Your child _______________ has just begun this spelling lesson. This week's test of words will be held on _______________.

Please contact me if you have any questions. Use the Comment Box to make any comments on your child's progress, noting any words that he or she still needs to review.

Sincerely,

____

Spelling Words

1. conviction
2. commanded
3. commonly
4. considered
5. continued
6. commander
7. commit
8. constitution
9. confusing
10. commence
11. commotion
12. commercial
13. communicate
14. communities
15. communication
16. committee

Home Activity

Think of a synonym or antonym for each Spelling Word. Give your child a synonym or an antonym and ask him or her to write the corresponding Spelling Word.

COMMENT BOX

NAME ______________________ CLASS ______________ DATE ______________

Lesson 21: Prefix *com-* (*con-*)

PRACTICE ACTIVITY

A. Find one misspelled Spelling Word in each sentence. Spell the words correctly on the lines.

Is this some form of comunication? ______________

Yes, you are comanded to find the hidden words. ______________

But it's so confuzing! ______________

It won't be once you comence. ______________

I've never concitered doing one of these! ______________

Try it! Our spelling commity thought it up. ______________

Add vowels to the group of letters to spell the Spelling Words. Remember that *y* can be used as a vowel.

cnvctn ______________

cmmtn ______________

cmmnct ______________

cmmt ______________

cmmnts ______________

cmmndr ______________

cnsttn ______________

cmmnl ______________

cmmrcl ______________

cntnd ______________

B. Write a paragraph on a topic of your choice. Use at least five Spelling Words.

____

____

____

____

____

____

____

Spelling Words

1. conviction
2. commanded
3. commonly
4. considered
5. continued
6. commander
7. commit
8. constitution
9. confusing
10. commence
11. commotion
12. commercial
13. communicate
14. communities
15. communication
16. committee

NAME ____________ CLASS ____________ DATE ____________

Lesson 22: Unstressed Ending *-ant/-ent*

WORD CARDS

absent	important	current	president
elephant	confident	instant	element
servant	excellent	opponent	permanent
assistant	innocent	significant	sufficient

Lesson 22: Unstressed Ending *-ant/-ent*

Dear Parent or Guardian,

Your child ______________________ has just begun this spelling lesson. This week's test of words will be held on

______________________________ .

Please contact me if you have any questions. Use the Comment Box to make any comments on your child's progress, noting any words that he or she still needs to review.

Sincerely,

____

Spelling Words

1. absent
2. important
3. current
4. president
5. elephant
6. confident
7. instant
8. element
9. servant
10. excellent
11. opponent
12. permanent
13. assistant
14. innocent
15. significant
16. sufficient

Home Activity

Prepare a list using the Spelling Words. Beginning with the second letter of each word, substitute a dash for every other letter. Give the list to your child, and ask him or her to finish spelling the words by filling in the blanks.

COMMENT BOX

NAME ______ CLASS ______ DATE ______

Lesson 22: Unstressed Ending *-ant/-ent*

PRACTICE ACTIVITY

A. Add vowels to the following groups of letters to make Spelling Words. Write the Spelling Words on the lines.

prsdnt ______

xcllnt ______

lphnt ______

bsnt ______

crrnt ______

ssstnt ______

sffcnt ______

cnfdnt ______

mprtnt ______

sgnfcnt ______

nncnt ______

prmnnt ______

ppnnt ______

srvnt ______

nstnt ______

lmnt ______

B. Write a paragraph on a topic of your choice. Use at least five Spelling Words.

______

______

______

______

______

______

______

______

______

______

______

Spelling Words

1. absent
2. important
3. current
4. president
5. elephant
6. confident
7. instant
8. element
9. servant
10. excellent
11. opponent
12. permanent
13. assistant
14. innocent
15. significant
16. sufficient

NAME CLASS DATE

Lesson 24: Patterns—More VCV Words

WORD CARDS

prison	linen	palace	climate
talent	novel	treason	comic
profit	token	weapon	gopher
pleasant	siren	frigid	spiral

Lesson 24: Patterns—More VCV Words

HOME ACTIVITY

Dear Parent or Guardian,

Your child _______________ has just begun this spelling lesson. This week's test of words will be held on _______________.

Please contact me if you have any questions. Use the Comment Box to make any comments on your child's progress, noting any words that he or she still needs to review.

Sincerely,

____

Spelling Words

1. prison
2. linen
3. palace
4. climate
5. talent
6. novel
7. treason
8. comic
9. profit
10. token
11. weapon
12. gopher
13. pleasant
14. siren
15. frigid
16. spiral

Home Activity

Ask your child to write an acrostic. Have your child write one of the Spelling Words. For each letter in the Spelling Word, have him or her write a phrase that starts with that letter. Encourage your child to do several acrostics each day.

COMMENT BOX

NAME ____________ CLASS ____________ DATE ____________

Lesson 24: Patterns—More VCV Words

PRACTICE ACTIVITY

A. Write the Spelling Word that answers each question.

Where does a king or queen live? ____________

What is another name for a comedian? ____________

What is a gun or a sword? ____________

What animal lives underground? ____________

What is a long fiction book called? ____________

What signals an alarm? ____________

Where are criminals kept? ____________

What goes on a mattress? ____________

What do businesspeople hope to make? ____________

What is the weather like at the North Pole? ____________

What is a small gift for a large favor? ____________

What does an actor need to succeed? ____________

What shape can a fancy stairway be? ____________

What might a spy commit? ____________

What is weather over a period of time? ____________

What would you call someone who is polite? ____________

B. Write a paragraph on a topic of your choice. Use at least five Spelling Words.

____

____

____

____

____

Spelling Words

1. prison
2. linen
3. palace
4. climate
5. talent
6. novel
7. treason
8. comic
9. profit
10. token
11. weapon
12. gopher
13. pleasant
14. siren
15. frigid
16. spiral

NAME CLASS DATE

Lesson 25: Mixed Spelling Patterns

WORD CARDS

banner	platform	hotel	funnel
habit	display	clever	gather
empty	chaos	suspense	Saturn
oval	orphan	fatal	crystal

Lesson 25: Mixed Spelling Patterns

HOME ACTIVITY

Dear Parent or Guardian,

Your child ______________________ has just begun this spelling lesson. This week's test of words will be held on ______________________.

Please contact me if you have any questions. Use the Comment Box to make any comments on your child's progress, noting any words that he or she still needs to review.

Sincerely,

____

Spelling Words

1. banner
2. platform
3. hotel
4. funnel
5. habit
6. display
7. clever
8. gather
9. empty
10. chaos
11. suspense
12. Saturn
13. oval
14. orphan
15. fatal
16. crystal

Home Activity

For each Spelling Word, write a sentence using the word. Read each sentence, leaving the Spelling Word out. Ask your child to write the Spelling Word that best fits the meaning of the sentence.

COMMENT BOX

NAME ______________________ CLASS ______________ DATE ______________

Lesson 25: Mixed Spelling Patterns

PRACTICE ACTIVITY

A. Write the Spelling Word that comes next alphabetically after each word.

gate ______________
band ______________
Oregon ______________
chair ______________
cry ______________
haberdasher ______________
clean ______________
hot ______________
out ______________
dish ______________
fat ______________
supper ______________
fun ______________
plate ______________
Saturday ______________
emperor ______________

B. Write a paragraph on a topic of your choice. Use at least five Spelling Words.

____
____
____
____
____
____
____
____
____
____
____

Spelling Words

1. banner
2. platform
3. hotel
4. funnel
5. habit
6. display
7. clever
8. gather
9. empty
10. chaos
11. suspense
12. Saturn
13. oval
14. orphan
15. fatal
16. crystal

NAME ______ CLASS ______ DATE ______

Lesson 26: Unusual Plurals

WORD CARDS

goldfish	trout	moose	cactus
media	fungi	bacteria	stimulus
stimuli	larvae	radius	nucleus
nuclei	species	salmon	hippopotamus

Lesson 26: Unusual Plurals

HOME ACTIVITY

Dear Parent or Guardian,

Your child ______________________ has just begun this spelling lesson. This week's test of words will be held on

____________________________________.

Please contact me if you have any questions. Use the Comment Box to make any comments on your child's progress, noting any words that he or she still needs to review.

Sincerely,

____

Spelling Words

1. goldfish
2. trout
3. moose
4. cactus
5. media
6. fungi
7. bacteria
8. stimulus
9. stimuli
10. larvae
11. radius
12. nucleus
13. nuclei
14. species
15. salmon
16. hippopotamus

Home Activity

Copy the list of Spelling Words, scrambling the letters in each word. Give the list to your child, and ask him or her to unscramble the lettters in each word so that the Spelling Words are spelled correctly.

COMMENT BOX

NAME ______ CLASS ______ DATE ______

Lesson 26: Unusual Plurals

PRACTICE ACTIVITY

A. Read the group of vowels for each Spelling Word. Write the word.

aiu ______
ou ______
ao ______
uei ______
ui ______
ooe ______
oi ______
iooau ______
ueu ______
aae ______
iuu ______
au ______
eia ______
eie ______
aeia ______
iui ______

B. Write a paragraph on a topic of your choice. Use at least five Spelling Words.

______

Spelling Words

1. goldfish
2. trout
3. moose
4. cactus
5. media
6. fungi
7. bacteria
8. stimulus
9. stimuli
10. larvae
11. radius
12. nucleus
13. nuclei
14. species
15. salmon
16. hippopotamus

NAME ______ CLASS ______ DATE ______

Lesson 27: Adjective Suffixes *-ive, -ous*

WORD CARDS

positive	attractive	effective	various
curious	tremendous	enormous	obvious
delicious	mysterious	executive	creative
fabulous	legislative	negative	sensitive

Lesson 27: Adjective Suffixes *-ive, -ous*

HOME ACTIVITY

Dear Parent or Guardian,

Your child ______________________ has just begun this spelling lesson. This week's test of words will be held on

______________________________ .

Please contact me if you have any questions. Use the Comment Box to make any comments on your child's progress, noting any words that he or she still needs to review.

Sincerely,

____

Spelling Words

1. positive
2. attractive
3. effective
4. various
5. curious
6. tremendous
7. enormous
8. obvious
9. delicious
10. mysterious
11. executive
12. creative
13. fabulous
14. legislative
15. negative
16. sensitive

Home Activity

Think of a question for each Spelling Word. For example, you might ask, "Which Spelling Word describes something very tasty?" *(delicious)* Have your child say and spell the correct Spelling Word.

COMMENT BOX

NAME ______________________ CLASS ______________ DATE ______________

Lesson 27: Adjective Suffixes *-ive, -ous*

PRACTICE ACTIVITY

A. Write the Spelling Word that is related to each word below.

mystery ______________

legislature ______________

sensation ______________

variation ______________

attraction ______________

enormity ______________

execute ______________

obviously ______________

curiosity ______________

effect ______________

position ______________

creation ______________

delicate ______________

negate ______________

fable ______________

tremble ______________

B. Write a paragraph on a topic of your choice. Use at least five Spelling Words.

Spelling Words

1. positive
2. attractive
3. effective
4. various
5. curious
6. tremendous
7. enormous
8. obvious
9. delicious
10. mysterious
11. executive
12. creative
13. fabulous
14. legislative
15. negative
16. sensitive

NAME CLASS DATE

Lesson 28: Words with Prefixes/Suffixes

WORD CARDS

unlikely	repayment	reaction	replacement
unpredictable	disagreement	renewal	unemployment
unexpectedly	unfortunately	unusually	reproduction
reconstruction	disagreeable	unsuccessful	uncomfortable

Lesson 28: Words with Prefixes/Suffixes

HOME ACTIVITY

Dear Parent or Guardian,

Your child ______________________ has just begun this spelling lesson. This week's test of words will be held on

______________________.

Please contact me if you have any questions. Use the Comment Box to make any comments on your child's progress, noting any words that he or she still needs to review.

Sincerely,

____

Spelling Words

1. unlikely
2. repayment
3. reaction
4. replacement
5. unpredictable
6. disagreement
7. renewal
8. unemployment
9. unexpectedly
10. unfortunately
11. unusually
12. reproduction
13. reconstruction
14. disagreeable
15. unsuccessful
16. uncomfortable

Home Activity

Prepare a flashcard for each Spelling Word. Show your child each card for a few seconds and then place it facedown on the table. Ask your child to spell the word you just showed him or her.

COMMENT BOX

NAME ________________ CLASS ________________ DATE ________________

Lesson 28: Words with Prefixes/Suffixes

PRACTICE ACTIVITY

A. Write the Spelling Word that is related to each word below.

usual ________________

new ________________

agreement ________________

success ________________

pay ________________

expect ________________

construct ________________

predict ________________

place ________________

act ________________

like ________________

produce ________________

agreeable ________________

comfort ________________

employ ________________

fortune ________________

B. Write a paragraph on a topic of your choice. Use at least five Spelling Words.

____

____

____

____

____

____

____

____

____

____

____

____

Spelling Words

1. *unlikely*
2. *repayment*
3. *reaction*
4. *replacement*
5. *unpredictable*
6. *disagreement*
7. *renewal*
8. *unemployment*
9. *unexpectedly*
10. *unfortunately*
11. *unusually*
12. *reproduction*
13. *reconstruction*
14. *disagreeable*
15. *unsuccessful*
16. *uncomfortable*

NAME ____________________ CLASS ____________ DATE ____________

Lesson 30: Suffixes in Combination

WORD CARDS

carefully	ownership	faithfully	peacefully
wonderfully	thoughtfully	relationship	respectively
naturally	nervously	gracefully	actively
joyfully	beautifully	successfully	accidentally

Lesson 30: Suffixes in Combination

HOME ACTIVITY

Dear Parent or Guardian,

Your child ______________________ has just begun this spelling lesson. This week's test of words will be held on

______________________.

Please contact me if you have any questions. Use the Comment Box to make any comments on your child's progress, noting any words that he or she still needs to review.

Sincerely,

____

Spelling Words

1. carefully
2. ownership
3. faithfully
4. peacefully
5. wonderfully
6. thoughtfully
7. relationship
8. respectively
9. naturally
10. nervously
11. gracefully
12. actively
13. joyfully
14. beautifully
15. successfully
16. accidentally

Home Activity

Prepare a list using the Spelling Words. Beginning with the second letter of each word, substitute a dash for every other letter. Give the list to your child, and ask him or her to finish spelling the words by filling in the blanks.

COMMENT BOX

NAME ____________ CLASS ____________ DATE ____________

Lesson 30: Suffixes in Combination

PRACTICE ACTIVITY

A. These words do not exist. In each case, one suffix is wrong. Substitute the correct suffix to make one of the Spelling Words. Then write the word on the line.

carefulwise ____________

joyulently ____________

successfulwise ____________

wonderosely ____________

respectiveways ____________

peaceosely ____________

gracefulwise ____________

ownertude ____________

beautiously ____________

nervefully ____________

thoughtfulwise ____________

relationdom ____________

naturicly ____________

accidentalways ____________

faithously ____________

actaciously ____________

B. Write a paragraph on a topic of your choice. Use at least five Spelling Words.

Spelling Words

1. carefully
2. ownership
3. faithfully
4. peacefully
5. wonderfully
6. thoughtfully
7. relationship
8. respectively
9. naturally
10. nervously
11. gracefully
12. actively
13. joyfully
14. beautifully
15. successfully
16. accidentally

NAME ______ CLASS ______ DATE ______

Lesson 31: Prefix *in-* (*im-*, *il-*, *ir-*)

WORD CARDS

incomplete	informal	incorrect	independent
illegal	impolite	impossible	invisible
irregular	inexpensive	impure	inability
impatient	indigestion	indefinite	incredible

Lesson 31: Prefix *in- (im-, il-, ir-)*

HOME ACTIVITY

Dear Parent or Guardian,

Your child ______________________ has just begun this spelling lesson. This week's test of words will be held on ______________________.

Please contact me if you have any questions. Use the Comment Box to make any comments on your child's progress, noting any words that he or she still needs to review.

Sincerely,

____

Spelling Words

1. *incomplete*
2. *informal*
3. *incorrect*
4. *independent*
5. *illegal*
6. *impolite*
7. *impossible*
8. *invisible*
9. *irregular*
10. *inexpensive*
11. *impure*
12. *inability*
13. *impatient*
14. *indigestion*
15. *indefinite*
16. *incredible*

Home Activity

Ask your child to create a crossword puzzle using the Spelling Words. Your child can use either the definition or a synonym of each Spelling Word to write the clues.

COMMENT BOX

NAME ______ CLASS ______ DATE ______

Lesson 31: Prefix *in-* (*im-*, *il-*, *ir-*)

PRACTICE ACTIVITY

A. Do the word search puzzle. Then write the words according to where you found them.

```
s k i n c i m p o s a t v
t i c s i n v i s i b l e
i f n m p c i n i i g i r
b m x e i o s d r n e n t
i o p r x m i e i d x c o
l m c e i p b p s e p o i
l b p g r l e e t f e r n
e a i u f e l n f i n r x
g t n l r t n d s n s e p
a i m a o e m e o i i c i
l o i r n m i n r t v t n
i n a b i l i t y e a e s
a s i r r e g u l a r g a
```

Across	Down	Diagonal
______	______	______
______	______	______
______	______	
	______	
	______	

If you use six of the letters from the word *considerate,* you can spell the word *ration.* Look at these words. Write the Spelling Word that has the letters needed to make the word.

cried ______ sting ______

limit ______ patent ______

bless ______ moral ______

B. Write a paragraph on a topic of your choice. Use at least five Spelling Words.

______

______

______

______

______

Spelling Words

1. incomplete
2. informal
3. incorrect
4. independent
5. illegal
6. impolite
7. impossible
8. invisible
9. irregular
10. inexpensive
11. impure
12. inability
13. impatient
14. indigestion
15. indefinite
16. incredible

NAME ____________________ CLASS ____________________ DATE ____________________

Lesson 32: Roots *-scrib-/-script-, -spect-*

WORD CARDS

inspect	suspect	scribe	script
descriptive	description	prescribed	inspector
spectacle	spectacular	scribbled	inscription
subscription	spectrum	spectators	transcripts

Lesson 32: Roots *-scrib-/-script-*, *-spect-*

HOME ACTIVITY

Dear Parent or Guardian,

Your child ______________________ has just begun this spelling lesson. This week's test of words will be held on

______________________.

Please contact me if you have any questions. Use the Comment Box to make any comments on your child's progress, noting any words that he or she still needs to review.

Sincerely,

____

Spelling Words

1. inspect
2. suspect
3. scribe
4. script
5. descriptive
6. description
7. prescribed
8. inspector
9. spectacle
10. spectacular
11. scribbled
12. inscription
13. subscription
14. spectrum
15. spectators
16. transcripts

Home Activity

For each Spelling Word, write a sentence using the word. Read each sentence, leaving out the Spelling Word. Ask your child to write the Spelling Word that best fits the meaning of the sentence.

COMMENT BOX

NAME ____________ CLASS ____________ DATE ____________

Lesson 32: Roots *-scrib-/-script-*, *-spect-*

PRACTICE ACTIVITY

A. Complete the crossword puzzle with Spelling Words.

Across

1. people who watch
4. the colors we can see
7. ordered
8. an engraved message
9. a copy of a play
10. one who inspects
11. an account given in words
14. amazing to behold

Down

1. one who writes by hand
2. written in a hasty way
3. described in a colorful way
4. one accused
5. an agreement to pay for magazines
6. exact copies of official records
12. something grand or showy
13. to look over carefully

B. Write a paragraph on a topic of your choice. Use at least five Spelling Words.

____

____

____

____

____

____

____

____

Spelling Words

1. inspect
2. suspect
3. scribe
4. script
5. descriptive
6. description
7. prescribed
8. inspector
9. spectacle
10. spectacular
11. scribbled
12. inscription
13. subscription
14. spectrum
15. spectators
16. transcripts

NAME ____________ CLASS ____________ DATE ____________

Lesson 33: Roots *-rupt-, -ject-*

WORD CARDS

objected	projected	objections	projections
erupt	abrupt	bankrupt	inject
disrupting	disruption	eject	reject
rejected	rupture	corrupt	interrupt

Lesson 33: Roots *-rupt-, -ject-*

Dear Parent or Guardian,

Your child ______________________ *has just begun this spelling lesson. This week's test of words will be held on* ______________________ .

Please contact me if you have any questions. Use the Comment Box to make any comments on your child's progress, noting any words that he or she still needs to review.

Sincerely,

____

Spelling Words

1. objected
2. projected
3. objections
4. projections
5. erupt
6. abrupt
7. bankrupt
8. inject
9. disrupting
10. disruption
11. eject
12. reject
13. rejected
14. rupture
15. corrupt
16. interrupt

Home Activity

Prepare a simple definition for each Spelling Word. Read the definition, and ask your child to write the Spelling Word that corresponds to the definition.

COMMENT BOX

NAME ______ CLASS ______ DATE ______

Lesson 33: Roots *-rupt-*, *-ject-*

PRACTICE ACTIVITY

A. Unscramble the following to find Spelling Words. Write the Spelling Words on the lines.

cretej ______

jectedob ______

brutap ______

turrpoc ______

tupingsrid ______

printerut ______

jctine ______

rjcinspoeto ______

dtjeeerc ______

ceejt ______

sonijobtec ______

jetcedorp ______

eptru ______

bkrunatp ______

dursnpitoi ______

prrtueu ______

B. Write a paragraph on a topic of your choice. Use at least five Spelling Words.

______

______

______

______

______

______

______

______

______

______

______

Spelling Words

1. *objected*
2. *projected*
3. *objections*
4. *projections*
5. *erupt*
6. *abrupt*
7. *bankrupt*
8. *inject*
9. *disrupting*
10. *disruption*
11. *eject*
12. *reject*
13. *rejected*
14. *rupture*
15. *corrupt*
16. *interrupt*

Answer Key for Practice Activities

p. 91 | Lesson 1: Short Vowels

A. ACROSS: 1. splendid, 5. contact, 7. rapid, 9. sack, 10. impulse, 11. summit, 12. depth, 14. glance, 15. contract; DOWN: 1. sketch, 2. nonsense, 3. comment, 4. liquid, 6. advance, 8. admit, 13. ethnic

B. *(Answers will vary.)*

p. 94 | Lesson 2: Long Vowels

A. slice, squeeze, thigh, peach, bait, prime, roast, praise, bride, breathe, globe, slope

grove, gross, stroke, spike

B. *(Answers will vary.)*

p. 97 | Lesson 3: Variant Vowels

A. proof, launched, cross, saucer, count, crawled, pounds, salt, account, youth, county, thousands, rumors, mountain, amount, shout

B. *(Answers will vary.)*

p. 100 | Lesson 4: Vowels Before *r*

A. scarce, reward, warrant, burnt, roar, purse, nervous, nightmare, apart, inserts, curb, source, declare, worse, turtle, sparkling

B. *(Answers will vary.)*

p. 103 | Lesson 6: Other Vowel Spellings

A. straight, boulder, dough, sleigh, rough

young, biscuit, though, busy, building, among, eighth, system, although, enough, courage

B. *(Answers will vary.)*

p. 106 | Lesson 7: Words with *ie* and *ei*

A. ACROSS: 3. receiver 8. mischief 9. freight 10. fierce 12. girlfriend 14. belief 15. pier 16. heights; DOWN: 1. weighed 2. boyfriend 4. receive 5. thieves 6. achieve 7. relief 11. reins 13. foreign

B. *(Answers will vary.)*

p. 109 | Lesson 8: Compound Words

A. fun-loving, barefoot, middle-aged, mean-spirited, upright

fireworks, seashore, fairy tales, thunderstorm

bedtime, cupboard, greenhouse

bodyguard, teenager

New Year

so-called

B. *(Answers will vary.)*

p. 112 | Lesson 9: Homophones

A. creek, week; creak, weak; sore; stake; steak; weather; steal; whether; steel; groan; soar; guest; guessed; grown

B. *(Answers will vary.)*

p. 115 | Lesson 10: Easily Confused Words

A. adopt, affect, angel, custom, later, latter, devise

angle, costume, device, descent, decent, accept, adapt, except, effect

B. *(Answers will vary.)*

p. 118 | Lesson 12: Changing *y* to *i*

A. identified, varied, industries, colonies, cities, activities, qualified, enemies, mummies, families, occupied, centuries, denied, supplies, allied, applies

B. *(Answers will vary.)*

p. 121 | Lesson 13: Endings /ər/, /əl/, /ən/

A. speaker, critical, original, German, layer, reader, Roman, beaten, political, stretcher, American, musical, criminal, Indian, rotten, explorer

B. *(Answers will vary.)*

p. 124 | Lesson 14: Patterns—VC/CV Words

A. gotten, frantic, engine, further, velvet, instinct, index, pillow, insist, indeed, escape, convince, intense, fifteen, monster, admire

B. *(Answers will vary.)*

p. 127 | Lesson 15: Patterns—V/CV Words

A. eager, fiber, evil, apron, basis, meter, Friday, scenic, razor, agent, rival, local, vital, motive, famous, cheetah

B. *(Answers will vary.)*

p. 130 | Lesson 16: Adding *-ed* and *-ing*

A. threatened, healed, answered, speaking, pointed, wondered, referring, returned, bragged,

Answer Key for Practice Activities *(continued)*

preferred, admitted, committed, scrubbed, lifted, spelling, cooling

B. *(Answers will vary.)*

p. 133 | Lesson 18: Noun Suffix *-ance/-ence*

A. entrance, importance, obedience, appearance, presence, difference, allowance, conference, insurance, intelligence, assurance, independence, instance, absence, ambulance, audience

B. *(Answers will vary.)*

p. 136 | Lesson 19: Suffixes *-ship, -ment, -ity*

A. championship, electricity, necessity, partnership, argument, curiosity, authority, statement, leadership, majority, activity, personality, ability, community, responsibility, friendship

B. *(Answers will vary.)*

p. 139 | Lesson 20: Prefix *ad- (ac-, as-, af-, ap-)*

A. ACROSS: 4. affection 5. accuse 6. apparent 9. approach 12. assembly 13. accustomed 14. accident 15. assign 16. assistance;
DOWN: 1. appointed 2. accurate 3. affair 7. applause 8. association 10. accompany 11. appreciate

B. *(Answers will vary.)*

p. 142 | Lesson 21: Prefix *com- (con-)*

A. communication, commanded, confusing, commence, considered, committee

conviction, commotion, communicate, commit, communities, commander, constitution, commonly, commercial, continued

B. *(Answers will vary.)*

p. 145 | Lesson 22: Unstressed Ending *-ant/-ent*

A. president, excellent, elephant, absent, current, assistant, sufficient, confident, important, significant, innocent, permanent, opponent, servant, instant, element

B. *(Answers will vary.)*

p. 148 | Lesson 24: Patterns—More VCV Words

A. palace, comic, weapon, gopher, novel, siren, prison, linen, profit, frigid, token, talent, spiral, treason, climate, pleasant

B. *(Answers will vary.)*

p. 151 | Lesson 25: Mixed Spelling Patterns

A. gather, banner, orphan, chaos, crystal, habit, clever, hotel, oval, display, fatal, suspense, funnel, platform, Saturn, empty

B. *(Answers will vary.)*

p. 154 | Lesson 26: Unusual Plurals

A. radius, trout, salmon, nuclei, fungi, moose, goldfish, hippopotamus, nucleus, larvae, stimulus, cactus, media, species, bacteria, stimuli

B. *(Answers will vary.)*

p. 157 | Lesson 27: Adjective Suffixes *-ive, -ous*

A. mysterious, legislative, sensitive, various, attractive, enormous, executive, obvious, curious, effective, positive, creative, delicious, negative, fabulous, tremendous

B. *(Answers will vary.)*

p. 160 | Lesson 28: Words with Prefixes/Suffixes

A. unusually, renewal, disagreement, unsuccessful, repayment, unexpectedly, reconstruction, unpredictable, replacement, reaction, unlikely, reproduction, disagreeable, uncomfortable, unemployment, unfortunately

B. *(Answers will vary.)*

p. 163 | Lesson 30: Suffixes in Combination

A. carefully, joyfully, successfully, wonderfully, respectively, peacefully, gracefully, ownership, beautifully, nervously, thoughtfully, relationship, naturally, accidentally, faithfully, actively

B. *(Answers will vary.)*

Answer Key for Practice Activities *(continued)*

p. 166 | Lesson 31: Prefix *in- (im-, il-, ir-)*

A. ACROSS: invisible, inability, irregular;
DOWN: illegal, incomplete, independent, indefinite, incorrect;
DIAGONAL: inexpensive, impure

incredible, impolite, impossible, indigestion, impatient, informal

B. *(Answers will vary.)*

p. 169 | Lesson 32: Roots *-scrib-/ -script-, -spect-*

A. ACROSS: 1. spectators 4. spectrum 7. prescribed 8. inscription 9. script 10. inspector 11. description 14. spectacular;
DOWN: 1. scribe 2. scribbled 3. descriptive 4. suspect 5. subscription 6. transcripts 12. spectacle 13. inspect

B. *(Answers will vary.)*

p. 172 | Lesson 33: Roots *-rupt-, -ject-*

A. reject, objected, abrupt, corrupt, disrupting, interrupt, inject, projections, rejected, eject, objections, projected, erupt, bankrupt, disruption, rupture

B. *(Answers will vary.)*

Teacher Resources

This section of the Teacher's Guide contains the following useful information.

Cumulative Word List
This section presents a comprehensive list of all words taught in *Spelling*. For each word, the grade level and the number of the lesson in which it is instructed are included.

Scope and Sequence
The chart in this section identifies the grade levels at which specific spelling strategies and skills are developed.

Bibliography
This bibliography includes informative professional articles and books about how students develop spelling proficiency as well as how they acquire related literacy skills. It also suggests a number of books for students.

Index
This index includes a useful list of major skills and activities.

Cumulative Word List for Grades 6–8

This alphabetical list of 1,406 words includes all the spelling words that appear in Grades 6–8 of *Spelling*. Each word in the list is followed by two numbers. The first number indicates the grade in which the word appears. The second number indicates the lesson. Therefore, the listing "abrupt 6 33" indicates that the word *abrupt* appears in Grade 6, lesson 33.

Word	Lesson	
abilities	8	3
ability	6	19
abolished	8	17
abrupt	6	33
absence	6	18
absent	6	22
absolute	8	17
abstract	8	17
accelerate	7	10
acceleration	7	33
accent	7	10
accept	6	10
acceptable	8	31
acceptance	8	31
accepted	7	10
access	8	5
accident	6	20
accidentally	6	30
accommodate	7	10
accompany	6	20
accompanying	7	10
accomplish	7	10
accomplished	8	6
account	6	3
accumulation	7	33
accurate	6	20
accuse	6	20
accustomed	6	20
achieve	6	7
acquired	8	3
actively	6	30
activities	6	12
activity	6	19
adapt	6	10
adjective	7	29
adjust	8	31
adjustments	8	31
administration	7	33
admire	6	14
admit	6	1
admits	7	22
admitted	6	16
adopt	6	10
advance	6	1
adventure	7	34
advertise	7	18
advice	8	6
advise	7	20
advocate	8	18
affair	6	20
affect	6	10
affection	6	20
affectionate	8	6
Africa	7	9
African	7	9
agent	6	15
agreeable	8	6
agricultural	7	33
aimlessly	8	35
allied	6	12
alligator	7	4
allowance	6	18
alphabet	8	11
although	6	6
altimeter	8	28
altitude	8	28
alto	8	28
amateur	8	8
ambulance	6	18
American	6	13
among	6	6
amount	6	3
analogy	7	32
analyze	7	18
anecdote	8	5
angel	6	10
angle	6	10
announced	7	10
announcement	8	6
annoy	7	10
answered	6	16
antidote	8	5
antique	7	23
apart	6	4
apologizing	7	32
apparent	6	20
appearance	6	18
applause	6	20
applicable	8	33
applies	6	12
appoint	7	10
appointed	6	20
appreciate	6	20
approach	6	20
approaching	7	10
approve	7	10
approved	8	6
apron	6	15
archaeologist	8	26
archaic	8	26
architectural	8	35
architecture	8	11
archives	8	26
arctic	7	12
argument	6	19
arithmetic	8	11
aroma	8	11
arrange	7	10
arrangements	7	10
array	7	10
arrest	7	10
arrested	8	6
arrived	7	10
artist	7	35
aspirin	7	29
assembly	6	20
assign	6	20
assistance	6	20
assistant	6	22
association	6	20
assurance	6	18
asterisk	8	28
astronaut	7	27
astronauts	8	28
astronomer	7	27
astronomy	7	27
athletes	7	29
atmosphere	8	12
attendance	7	21
attended	8	31
attitude	7	15
attract	7	22
attractive	6	27
audience	6	18
Australia	7	9
Australian	7	9
authority	6	19
autobiography	7	33
autograph	7	27
automatically	8	26
automobile	7	30
automobiles	8	26
autumn	7	25
autumnal	7	25
awe	8	4
awesome	7	11
awful	8	4
awfully	8	4
awkward	7	11
backward	7	11
bacteria	6	26
bait	6	2
bakery	7	14
balance	7	21
ballet	7	23
banjo	7	5
bankrupt	6	33
banner	6	25
banquet	8	32
barbecue	8	27
bard	8	2
barefoot	6	8
barefooted	8	9
barometer	7	27
barred	8	2
barrier	7	15
basis	6	15
bazaar	8	5

Word	Lesson	
beaten	6	13
beautifully	6	30
bedtime	6	8
belief	6	7
berth	7	2
beverage	7	12
bicycle	7	28
binoculars	7	28
biography	7	27
biologist	7	35
biology	7	32
birth	7	2
biscuit	6	6
bizarre	8	5
blouse	8	8
boarder	8	2
bodyguard	6	8
booklet	8	32
border	8	2
bothering	7	3
boulder	6	6
boundary	7	12
bouquet	7	23
boycott	8	30
boyfriend	6	7
bracelet	8	32
bragged	6	16
Braille	8	30
breadth	8	5
breath	8	5
breathe	6	2
bride	6	2
brilliant	7	21
buffalo	7	15
buffet	7	23
bugle	7	5
building	6	6
burnt	6	4
burro	8	2
burrow	8	2
busy	6	6
cabinet	8	32
cactus	6	26
cafeteria	7	4
calculate	7	18
camouflage	7	23
capital	8	2
Capitol	8	2
caravan	7	30
carbohydrate	7	32
carefully	6	30
carelessly	8	35
cargo	8	27
carnival	8	27
carrying	7	3
cassette	8	32
catalog	7	32
caucus	8	34
celebrate	7	18
Celsius	8	30
centimeters	7	27
centuries	6	12
century	7	14
chairperson	7	1
champion	7	30
championship	6	19
chaos	6	25
characteristic	7	33
chattering	8	21
chauffeur	8	8
cheating	7	3
cheetah	6	15
chemical	8	12
childish	7	11
chili	7	4
chipmunk	8	27
chocolate	7	29
chorus	8	11
chute	7	2
cinnamon	7	15
circles	7	16
circuit	8	25
circular	7	16
circulation	8	25
circumference	8	25
circumstances	8	25
cities	6	12
civilian	7	35
clarinet	7	5
classical	7	5
clever	6	25
climate	6	24
cocoa	7	4
colonial	7	24
colonies	6	12
colony	7	24
combination	8	15
combine	8	15
comic	6	24
commanded	6	21
commander	6	21
commence	6	21
comment	6	1
commercial	6	21
commit	6	21
commitment	7	22
committed	6	16
committee	6	21
commonly	6	21
commotion	6	21
communicate	6	21
communication	6	21
communities	6	21
community	6	19
companion	7	24
company	7	24
compelled	7	3
complicated	8	33
composer	7	5
composition	7	20
compromise	7	18
concentrate	8	18
concert	7	5
conducted	8	31
conductor	7	5
confederate	8	9
conference	6	18
confidence	7	21
confident	6	22
confined	8	33
confusing	6	21
congratulate	7	18
conjunction	8	33
conscience	8	5
conscious	8	5
conservation	8	14
considered	6	21
constant	7	21
constitution	6	21
constructing	7	20
contact	6	1
contained	8	3
container	8	31
contented	8	9
continue	8	4
continued	6	21
continuous	8	4
continuously	8	4
contract	6	1
contracted	7	22
controlling	7	3
convention	7	34
conviction	6	21
convince	6	14
cooling	6	16
cooperate	7	18
cooperation	7	33
corral	7	4
corridor	7	15
corrupt	6	33
cosmonauts	8	28
costume	6	10
count	6	3
county	6	3
coup	8	8
coupon	7	23
courage	6	6
coyote	7	4
crawled	6	3
creak	6	9
creative	6	27
creek	6	9
criminal	6	13
critical	6	13
criticism	8	22
criticize	7	18
crochet	8	8
crooked	8	9
croquet	8	8
cross	6	3
cruelty	8	22
crystal	6	25
cupboard	6	8
curb	6	4
curiosity	6	19
curious	6	27
current	6	22
custom	6	10
cycle	8	10
cyclone	8	10
daylight	7	1
debate	8	18
debris	8	8
decade	7	28
decay	7	8
deceived	8	31
December	7	28
decent	6	10
decimal	7	28
declare	6	4
decline	7	8
decorate	8	18
deduction	7	8
defeat	7	8
defects	7	8
definitely	8	33
dehydrated	7	32
delegate	8	18
delicious	6	27
democratic	8	9

Word	Lesson	
demonstrate	8	18
denied	6	12
dependent	7	8
depends	7	34
depositing	7	20
depot	8	8
depth	6	1
descent	6	10
description	6	32
descriptive	6	32
designated	7	25
designed	7	25
despair	8	4
desperate	7	29
desperately	8	4
destroyed	7	8
destruction	7	20
detained	8	31
device	6	10
devise	6	10
dialogue	7	23
diameter	7	27
dictator	8	14
dictionaries	8	14
dictionary	7	14
difference	6	18
different	7	12
diplomacy	7	24
diplomatic	7	24
disabled	7	8
disadvantages	7	8
disagreeable	6	28
disagreement	6	28
disappeared	7	8
disappointment	7	8
disastrous	7	29
discovered	7	8
discovery	7	14
disguise	7	8
diskette	8	32
disliked	7	8
dismissed	7	22
display	6	25
dispose	7	8
disposed	8	15
disposition	8	15
disrupting	6	33
disruption	6	33
dissolved	7	8
distract	7	22
distribute	8	15
distribution	8	15
documentary	7	14
doubt	7	17
doubtful	7	17
doubtless	7	17
dough	6	6
drama	8	4
dramatic	8	4
dramatically	8	4
drowned	7	29
duplicate	8	33
eager	6	15
economically	8	35
ecstatic	7	29
editor	7	24
editorial	7	24
educate	8	31
effect	6	10
effective	6	27
eighth	6	6
eject	6	33
electrical	8	12
electricity	6	19
electronic	8	9
elegant	7	21
element	6	22
elephant	6	22
eliminate	8	18
elite	8	8
embarrassed	8	8
embassy	8	21
emigrate	8	14
empty	6	25
enclose	7	7
encourage	7	7
encyclopedia	7	33
endurance	7	21
enemies	6	12
engine	6	14
engineer	7	35
England	7	9
English	7	9
enjoying	7	7
enormous	6	27
enough	6	6
enthusiasm	7	7
entrance	6	18
envelope	7	7
environment	8	12
episode	8	11
equality	8	20
equation	8	20
equator	8	20
equivalent	8	20
erupt	6	33
escape	6	14
especially	7	17
estimate	8	18
ethnic	6	1
eventually	8	35
evergreen	8	1
evil	6	15
exaggerated	8	21
examination	7	30
exceed	7	7
excel	7	7
excellent	6	22
except	6	10
exceptionally	7	33
excess	8	5
exchange	7	7
excitement	7	7
exclaim	7	7
exclude	7	7
executive	6	27
exercise	7	18
existence	7	21
exit	7	7
expand	7	7
experience	7	21
experiments	8	12
explode	7	7
explorer	6	13
exported	8	14
express	7	7
extend	7	7
extraordinary	8	17
extraterrestrial	8	17
extravagant	8	17
fabulous	6	27
factory	7	14
Fahrenheit	8	30
fairy tales	6	8
faithfully	6	30
familiar	7	24
families	6	12
family	7	24
famous	6	15
fantastic	7	24
fantasy	7	24
fatal	6	25
fatigue	7	23
favorably	8	35
February	7	12
feminine	7	11
feudal	8	5
fiber	6	15
fiddle	7	5
fierce	6	7
fifteen	6	14
finally	8	5
financial	8	33
finely	8	5
fireworks	6	8
following	7	3
foolish	7	11
forbidding	8	3
foreign	6	7
formation	7	34
formula	7	34
fortunate	7	17
fortunately	8	35
fortune	7	17
foul	8	2
fowl	8	2
France	7	9
frankfurter	8	30
frantic	6	14
freight	6	7
French	7	9
frequent	7	21
Friday	6	15
friendship	6	19
frigid	6	24
fungi	6	26
fun-loving	6	8
funnel	6	25
further	6	14
furthermore	8	1
futile	8	5
gallery	7	15
gasoline	7	30
gather	6	25
gathered	7	3
generation	8	10
generator	8	10
genes	8	10
genius	8	10
genuine	7	11
geographic	8	28
geography	7	27
geology	8	28
geometry	8	28
German	6	13
gingerbread	8	1
girlfriend	6	7
glance	6	1
globe	6	2
goalie	7	35

Word	Lesson	
goldfish	6	26
good-natured	8	1
gopher	6	24
gorilla	7	15
gotten	6	14
governmental	8	35
gracefully	6	30
grandparents	7	1
graph	7	27
grayish	7	11
Greece	7	9
Greek	7	9
greenhouse	6	8
greenish	7	11
groan	6	9
groaned	7	3
gross	6	2
grove	6	9
guardian	7	35
guessed	6	9
guest	6	9
guitar	7	4
gymnasium	7	30
habit	6	25
haiku	8	34
hamburger	8	30
hammered	7	3
handkerchief	8	1
handsome	7	11
harmony	7	5
harp	7	5
harpoon	8	34
harvesting	8	3
haste	7	25
hasten	7	25
headache	7	1
headquarters	8	1
healed	6	16
heart attack	8	1
heights	6	7
heir	7	25
hemisphere	8	12
heritage	7	25
heroes	8	11
heroic	8	27
hesitate	8	18
hibachi	8	34
hickory	8	27
hippopotamus	6	26
historian	7	35
historic	8	9
historical	7	24
historically	8	35
history	7	24
homemade	8	1
homesick	8	1
horrid	8	9
hotel	6	25
hurricane	7	15
hydrant	7	32
icicle	8	32
identification	7	33
identified	6	12
identity	7	29
igloo	8	34
illegal	6	31
illustrate	7	18
illustrated	8	6
immigration	8	14
impatient	6	31
impolite	6	31
importance	6	18
important	6	22
imported	8	14
impossible	6	31
impressed	8	6
improved	8	6
impulse	6	1
impure	6	31
inability	6	31
inaugurate	7	18
incident	7	21
incidentally	7	29
included	8	6
incomplete	6	31
incorrect	6	31
incredible	6	31
indeed	6	14
indefinite	6	31
independence	6	18
independent	6	13
index	6	14
Indian	6	13
indictment	8	14
indigestion	6	31
industries	6	12
inexpensive	6	31
infinite	8	33
influence	8	21
informal	6	31
inject	6	33
injury	7	14
innocent	6	22
inscription	6	32
inserts	6	4
insist	6	14
insisted	8	16
inspect	6	32
inspection	8	6
inspector	8	32
inspiration	7	34
inspired	7	34
instance	6	18
instant	6	22
instinct	6	14
instructions	7	20
instruments	8	12
insurance	6	18
intellectual	8	21
intelligence	6	18
intense	6	14
intercept	8	16
intermediate	8	16
international	8	16
interrupt	6	33
interrupted	8	16
interview	8	16
intramural	8	25
intrastate	8	25
introduction	8	25
introvert	8	25
invention	7	34
inventor	7	34
investigate	8	18
investigated	8	16
invisible	6	31
irregular	6	31
irresponsible	8	6
irrigated	8	6
ivory	7	29
jaguar	7	4
Japan	7	9
Japanese	7	9
jazz	7	5
jewelry	7	12
joyfully	6	30
judges	7	17
judgment	7	17
judicial	7	17
juncture	8	33
justice	8	31
justified	8	3
karate	8	34
kayak	8	34
killer whale	7	1
kilometers	7	27
kimono	8	34
kindergarten	8	34
laboratory	7	30
labored	7	3
labyrinth	8	11
landscape	8	27
large-scale	8	1
larvae	6	26
laser	8	12
later	6	10
latter	6	10
layer	6	13
leadership	6	19
leaflet	8	32
league	7	23
legislative	6	27
length	7	12
letting	7	3
librarian	7	35
library	7	12
life jackets	7	1
lifted	6	16
lightning	7	29
limousine	7	30
linen	6	24
liquid	6	1
listening	7	3
literature	7	12
local	6	15
logic	7	32
loneliness	8	35
lonesome	7	11
long-term	8	1
loudspeaker	8	1
loyalty	8	22
luncheon	7	30
luncheonette	8	32
luxury	7	14
macaroni	8	27
machinery	7	14
mackintosh	8	30
magnetic	8	9
magnificent	7	21
magnificently	8	20
magnify	8	20
magnitude	8	20
majority	6	19
malapropism	8	30
mammoth	8	34
mandate	8	18
marathon	8	11
marine	7	11
masculine	7	11
massacre	7	15

Word	Lesson	
mathematics	7	30
matinee	8	8
mean-spirited	6	8
mechanism	8	22
media	6	26
medicinal	8	15
medicine	8	15
melancholy	8	11
memorandum	7	30
memorize	7	18
mercury	8	30
metallic	8	9
meter	6	15
meters	7	27
metropolitan	8	26
microcomputer	8	20
microorganism	8	20
microphone	8	10
microscope	7	32
microscopic	8	20
microwave	8	20
middle-aged	6	8
migrate	8	14
mischief	6	7
misfortune	7	17
missed	7	2
missionary	7	14
mist	7	2
moccasins	7	15
molecules	8	12
monologue	7	32
monopoly	7	28
monotonous	7	28
monsoon	8	27
monster	6	14
moonlight	7	1
moose	6	26
mosquito	7	4
motive	6	15
mountain	6	3
multicolored	8	20
multicultural	8	20
multimedia	8	20
multiplication	8	20
multitude	8	20
mummies	6	12
muscle	7	16
muscular	7	16
musical	6	13
musician	7	35
mysterious	6	27
mysteriously	8	35
mythology	7	32
narrative	8	21
naturalization	8	35
naturally	6	30
nautical	8	28
navigation	8	28
necessary	7	20
necessity	6	19
necktie	7	30
negative	6	27
negotiate	8	18
nervous	6	14
nervously	6	30
New Year	6	8
nightmare	6	4
nonsense	6	1
novel	6	24
novelty	8	22

Word	Lesson	
nuclei	6	26
nucleus	6	26
nursery	7	14
nutrients	8	3
obedience	6	18
objected	6	33
objection	8	23
objections	6	33
objective	8	23
obligation	8	15
oblige	8	15
oblong	8	23
obscure	8	23
observation	8	23
observatory	8	14
obsessions	8	23
obstacle	8	23
obtained	8	23
obvious	6	27
obviously	8	23
occasionally	8	23
occupant	8	23
occupation	8	23
occupied	6	12
October	7	28
octopus	7	28
odometer	8	28
odyssey	8	30
offensive	8	23
offered	7	22
offering	8	23
offshore	7	1
omit	7	22
omitted	8	3
opera	8	27
opossum	7	15
opponent	6	22
opportunity	8	23
opposite	7	20
opposition	8	23
optic	8	26
optical	8	26
optimism	8	22
optometrist	8	26
organization	7	33
organize	7	18
original	6	13
orphan	6	25
oval	6	25
overnight	7	1
ownership	6	30
packet	8	32
pain	7	2
palace	6	24
palette	8	2
pallet	8	2
pamphlet	8	32
pane	7	2
parachute	7	30
paragraph	7	27
parakeet	8	27
parallel	8	21
paralyze	7	18
parka	8	34
participate	8	18
particle	8	32
particles	7	16
particular	7	16
partnership	6	19
passionate	8	9

Word	Lesson	
pasteurize	8	30
patio	7	4
patriotic	8	15
patriotism	8	22
patriots	8	15
peacefully	6	30
peacefulness	8	35
peach	6	2
pending	7	34
penetrate	7	29
penniless	8	21
perceived	8	31
perception	8	25
perfectly	8	25
perform	7	34
performance	7	5
perfume	8	8
perimeter	8	25
periodic	8	25
peripheral	8	25
periscope	7	32
permanent	6	22
permanently	8	25
permit	7	22
permitting	7	3
persecuted	8	5
persimmon	8	34
personality	6	19
perspective	8	25
persuaded	8	25
petrified	8	3
phenomenon	8	11
philosopher	8	26
philosophy	8	11
phonograph	8	10
phosphate	8	18
photograph	7	27
photography	7	27
physical	8	11
physician	7	35
pianist	7	5
piano	8	27
picnic basket	8	1
pier	6	7
pigeon	8	8
pillow	6	14
pinnacle	7	15
pioneer	7	35
plaque	7	23
plateau	8	8
platform	6	25
platinum	7	29
pleasant	6	24
pneumonia	8	11
poetic	8	9
pointed	6	16
policy	8	26
political	6	13
politician	7	35
politics	8	26
polluted	8	21
popular	7	16
population	7	16
portable	8	14
portrait	7	23
position	7	20
positive	6	27
possibility	7	33
potatoes	8	3
pounds	6	3

Word	Lesson	
poverty	8	22
prairie	7	23
praise	6	2
predicting	8	14
preferred	6	16
prejudice	7	17
prescribed	6	32
presence	6	18
preservation	8	14
president	6	22
pretzel	8	34
prime	6	2
principal	8	2
principle	8	2
prison	6	24
probability	8	12
probably	7	12
proceeds	8	16
produced	8	3
productive	8	31
profession	8	4
professionally	8	4
profit	6	24
profitable	8	16
programming	8	3
projected	6	33
projections	6	33
proof	6	3
propose	8	15
proposition	8	15
prosecuted	8	5
prosperity	8	16
protested	8	16
provisions	8	16
psychiatrist	7	35
psychology	7	32
purse	6	4
qualified	6	12
quart	7	28
quarters	7	28
quartet	7	28
radar	8	12
radius	6	26
ragged	8	9
rapid	6	1
razor	6	15
reaction	6	28
reader	6	13
real	7	2
realism	8	22
realize	7	18
receipt	7	25
receive	6	7
receiver	6	7
reception	7	25
recess	7	20
recognize	7	18
recommendation	7	33
reconstruction	6	28
rectangle	7	16
rectangular	7	16
recycle	8	10
reddish	7	11
reel	7	2
refer	7	22
reference	7	12
references	7	22
referring	6	16
refining	8	33
reform	7	34

Word	Lesson	
refrigerator	7	30
refused	8	3
regular	7	16
regulate	8	18
regulation	7	16
rehabilitation	7	33
rehearsal	7	5
reins	6	7
reject	6	33
rejected	6	33
relationship	6	30
relief	6	7
reluctant	7	21
renewal	6	28
repayment	6	28
repeated	8	15
repetition	8	15
replacement	6	28
reproduction	6	28
reservation	8	14
resign	7	25
resignation	7	25
resources	8	3
respectively	6	30
respiration	7	34
responsibilities	7	33
responsibility	6	19
restaurant	7	29
returned	6	16
revised	7	20
revolutionary	7	14
reward	6	4
rhythm	8	11
rhythmically	8	35
rigid	8	9
rival	6	15
rivalry	8	22
roar	6	4
roast	6	2
robbery	8	22
rodeo	7	4
Roman	6	13
rotten	6	13
rough	6	6
royalty	8	22
ruined	7	3
rumors	6	3
rupture	6	33
sack	6	1
sailboat	7	1
salmon	6	26
salt	6	3
sandwich	8	30
sapling	8	32
satellite	8	21
Saturn	6	25
saucer	6	3
scarce	6	4
scattering	8	21
scenery	7	14
scenic	6	15
scholarship	8	26
scholastic	8	26
scientist	7	35
scientists	8	12
scope	7	32
scribbled	6	32
scribe	6	32
script	6	32
scrubbed	6	16

Word	Lesson	
scuba	8	12
seashore	6	8
seaweed	7	1
seismometer	8	28
selfish	7	11
sensation	8	31
sensationally	8	35
sensitive	6	27
sensory	8	31
sentimental	8	31
separate	7	12
separating	8	3
sequoia	8	30
servant	6	22
shone	7	2
shoot	7	2
shout	6	3
shown	7	2
sign	7	25
signature	7	25
significant	6	22
significantly	8	35
simulate	8	18
simultaneously	7	33
siren	6	24
skeleton	8	27
sketch	6	1
sleigh	6	6
slice	6	2
slope	6	2
soar	6	9
so-called	6	8
softened	7	25
softly	7	25
sonar	8	12
sophisticated	8	26
sophomore	8	26
sore	6	9
source	6	4
spaghetti	8	27
Spain	7	9
Spanish	7	9
sparkling	6	4
speaker	6	13
speaking	6	16
specialist	7	17
specialty	8	22
species	6	26
specific	7	17
specifications	7	17
spectacle	6	32
spectacular	6	32
spectators	6	32
spectrum	6	32
spelling	6	16
spike	6	2
spiral	6	24
splendid	6	1
spoonerism	8	30
squeeze	6	2
stadium	8	11
stagecoach	8	1
stake	6	9
stampede	7	4
statement	6	19
stationary	8	2
stationery	8	2
statuette	8	32
steak	6	9
steal	6	9

Word	Lesson	
steel	6	9
stimuli	6	26
stimulus	6	26
straight	6	6
strain	8	4
strategic	7	24
strategy	7	24
strawberry	7	1
strength	7	12
strenuous	8	4
strenuously	8	4
stretcher	6	13
stroke	6	2
structures	7	20
studying	7	9
stupid	8	17
subdued	8	17
subjected	8	30
submarine	7	17
submerged	8	22
submit	7	3
submitted	8	32
subscription	6	21
substance	7	17
subtracting	8	22
subway	7	17
succeeded	8	20
successfully	7	30
suede	6	2
suffer	7	22
sufficient	7	22
suite	6	8
summit	8	1
summoned	6	21
supermarket	8	28
superpower	8	28
supervision	8	28
supplies	8	12
supply	6	20
supported	8	14
surgeon	8	8
suspect	8	32
suspended	6	34
suspense	7	25
swallowed	6	3
swayed	7	2
syllable	7	15
symbolic	7	10
sympathetic	8	10
symphony	8	10
symptoms	8	10
synonyms	8	10
synthetic	8	10
system	8	6
tablet	8	32
talent	6	24
technician	7	35
technique	7	23
technological	8	12
technology	7	32
teenager	6	8
teenagers	7	30

Word	Lesson	
telegram	8	16
telegraph	8	16
telephones	8	10
telescope	7	32
telescopes	8	16
televised	7	20
temperature	7	12
tentatively	7	29
terrace	8	33
terrific	8	21
territorial	8	33
territories	8	33
territory	7	14
thermometer	7	27
thieves	6	7
thigh	6	2
though	6	6
thoughtfully	6	30
thousands	6	3
threatened	6	16
thunderstorm	6	8
tide	7	2
tied	7	2
tobacco	7	15
toboggan	8	34
token	6	24
tomato	7	4
tomorrow	7	15
tornado	7	4
torrential	8	21
tortillas	7	4
tourism	8	22
transaction	8	17
transcripts	6	32
transfer	7	22
transferred	8	17
transformed	7	34
transient	8	17
translation	8	17
transmission	7	22
transportation	8	17
treason	6	24
treasury	7	14
tremendous	6	27
triangle	7	16
triangles	7	28
triangular	7	16
tricycle	7	28
triggered	8	21
trio	7	28
triple	7	28
trout	6	26
trumpet	7	5
tundra	8	34
turtle	6	4
tuxedo	8	30
twelfth	7	12
typewriter	7	1
umbrella	7	15
uncertainty	8	22
uncomfortable	6	28
underground	8	1

Word	Lesson	
underlying	8	16
underneath	8	16
undersized	8	9
undertake	8	16
underwater	7	1
undoubtedly	7	17
unemployment	6	28
unexpectedly	6	28
unfortunate	7	17
unfortunately	6	28
uniform	7	34
unique	7	23
universe	8	12
unlikely	6	28
unpredictable	6	28
unsuccessful	6	28
unusually	6	28
upright	6	8
uttered	8	21
vaccination	8	21
vague	7	23
vanilla	7	4
varied	6	12
various	6	27
vegetable	7	12
vehicles	7	16
vehicular	7	16
velvet	6	14
verdict	8	14
victory	7	14
Vietnam	7	9
Vietnamese	7	9
violin	7	5
vision	7	20
visitors	7	20
vital	6	15
vocabulary	8	33
vocal	8	33
vocational	8	33
volunteer	7	35
voyage	7	23
waffle	8	34
walrus	8	27
warrant	6	4
watermelon	7	1
weak	6	9
weapon	6	24
weather	6	9
week	6	9
weighed	6	7
well-wisher	8	1
whether	6	9
wholesome	7	11
wildlife	7	1
wondered	6	16
wonderfully	6	30
worse	6	4
yacht	8	27
yearling	8	32
young	6	6
youth	6	3
zeppelin	8	30

Scope and Sequence

	6	7	8
SPELLING GENERALIZATIONS			
Sound-Letter Relationships			
Consonants	✓	✓	✓
Consonant Digraphs	✓	✓	✓
Consonant Clusters	✓	✓	✓
Short Vowels	✓	✓	✓
Long Vowels	✓	✓	✓
Vowel Diphthongs/Vowel Digraphs/Variant Vowels	✓	✓	✓
R-Controlled Vowels	✓	✓	✓
Silent Letters	✓	✓	✓
Schwa	✓	✓	✓
Double Letters	✓	✓	✓
Spelling Patterns	✓	✓	✓
Word Structure			
Contractions	✓	✓	✓
Plurals/Possessives	✓	✓	✓
Inflected Forms/Comparatives/Superlatives	✓	✓	✓
Prefixes	✓	✓	✓
Suffixes	✓	✓	✓
Greek and Latin Word Parts	✓	✓	✓
Word Analysis			
Phonograms	✓	✓	✓
Compound Words	✓	✓	✓
Syllable Patterns	✓	✓	✓
Letter Patterns	✓	✓	✓
Pronunciation	✓	✓	✓

Scope and Sequence *(continued)*

	6	7	8
SPELLING STRATEGIES			
Rhyming Words	✓	✓	✓
Word Shapes	✓	✓	✓
Word Families	✓	✓	✓
How to Study a Word	✓	✓	✓
Picture/Sound Out a Word	✓	✓	✓
Related Words	✓	✓	✓
Mnemonic Devices	✓	✓	✓
Spell/Proofread with a Partner	✓	✓	✓
Try Different Spellings/Beat Guess	✓	✓	✓
Dictionary/Definitions	✓	✓	✓
Proofread Twice	✓	✓	✓
Apply Spelling Rules	✓	✓	✓
VOCABULARY DEVELOPMENT			
Classify/Categorize Words	✓	✓	✓
Antonyms	✓	✓	✓
Content-Area Words	✓	✓	✓
Synonyms	✓	✓	✓
Homophones	✓	✓	✓
Multiple Meanings/Homographs	✓	✓	✓
Dictionary (for meaning)	✓	✓	✓
Word Origins	✓	✓	✓
Analogies	✓	✓	✓
Idioms	✓	✓	✓
Denotation/Connotation	✓	✓	✓
Parts of Speech	✓	✓	✓
Root Words	✓	✓	✓
WRITING			
Proofreading	✓	✓	✓
Frequently Misspelled Words	✓	✓	✓

Bibliography

Professional List for Teachers

Bear, Donald R. "'Learning to Fasten the Seat of My Union Suit Without Looking Around': The Synchrony of Literacy Development." *Theory Into Practice* 30, No. 3 (Summer 1991): 149–157.

Bear, Donald R., and Diane Barone. "Using Children's Spelling to Group for Word Study and Directed Reading in the Primary Classroom." *Reading Psychology: An International Quarterly* 10 (1989): 275–292.

Bolton, Faye, and Diane Snowball. *Teaching Spelling: A Practical Resource.* Portsmouth: Heinemann, 1993.

Buchanan, Ethel. *Spelling for Whole-Language Classrooms.* Winnipeg, Canada: 1992.

Chomsky, Carol. "Invented Spelling in the Open Classroom." New England Kindergarten Conference (1973): 499–518. Portions of this article first appeared in "Beginning Reading Through Invented Spelling" in *Quality Education Makes a Difference (1–8)* and are reprinted by permission of Lesley College.

Cunningham, Patricia M., and James W. Cunningham. "Making Words: Enhancing the Invented Spelling-Decoding Connection." *The Reading Teacher* 46 No. 2 (October 1992): 106–115.

Farr, Roger, Cheryl Kelleher, Katherine Lee, and Caroline Beverstock. "An Analysis of the Spelling Patterns of Children in Grades Two Through Eight: Study of a National Sample of Children's Writing." Center for Reading and Language Studies, Indiana University, 1990.

Fry, Edward, Ph.D. *Spelling Book: Words Most Needed Plus Phonics for Grades 1–6.* Laguna Beach, CA: Laguna Beach Educational Books, n.d.

Gentry, J. Richard. *SPEL . . . Is a Four-Letter Word.* Portsmouth: Heinemann, 1983.

Gill, J. Thomas Jr. "Focus on Research: Development of Word Knowledge as It Relates to Reading, Spelling, and Instruction." *Language Arts* 69 (October 1992): 444–453.

Goodman, Yetta M. "Language and the English Curriculum," *Education in the 80's: English.* Edited by R. Baird Shuman, n.p.: National Education Association, 1981.

Graves, Donald H. *Writing: Teachers and Children at Work.* Portsmouth: Heinemann, 1983.

Hillerich, Robert L. *Teaching Children to Write, K–8: A Complete Guide to Developing Writing Skills.* New York: Prentice-Hall, Inc., 1985. (excerpts)

Hodges, Richard E. *Learning to Spell.* Urbana, Illinois: ERIC Clearinghouse on Reading and Communication Skills and National Council of Teachers of English, 1981.

---. "The Conventions of Writing" in *Handbook of Research on Teaching the English Language Arts,* 775–786. n.p., 1991.

Holdaway, Don. "Shared Book Experience: Teaching Reading Using Favorite Books." *In Early Literacy: A Constructivist Foundation for Whole Language.* Edited by Constance Kamiij, Maryann Manning, and Gary Manning, 91–109. n.p. National Education Association, 1991.

Jongsma, Kathleen Stumpf. "Reading-Spelling Links." *The Reading Teacher* (April 1990): 608–610.

---. "Editorial Comment: Developmental Spelling Theory Revisited." *Reading Psychology: An International Quarterly* 10 (1989): iii–x.

Loomer, Bradley M. *Spelling Research: The Most Commonly Asked Questions About Spelling . . . And What the Research Says.* Mt. Vernon, Iowa: Useful Learning, 1990.

McAlexander, Patricia J., Ann B. Dobie, and Noel Gregg. *Beyond the "SP" Label: Improving the Spelling of Learning Disabled and Basic Writers.* National Council of Teachers of English, 1992.

Morris, Darrell. "The Relationship Between Children's Concept of Word in Text and Phoneme Awareness in Learning to Read: A Longitudinal Study." *Research in the Teaching of English* 27, No. 2 (May 1993): 132–154.

---. "'Word Sort': A Categorization Strategy for Improving Word Recognition Ability." *Reading Psychology: An International Quarterly* 3: (1982): 247–259.

Routman, Regie. *Invitations: Changing as Teachers and Learners K–12.* Portsmouth: Heinemann, 1991. (excerpts)

---. "'The Uses and Abuses of Invented Spelling." *Instructor* (May/June 1992): 418–424.

Schlagal, Robert C., and Joy Harris Schlagal. "The Integral Character of Spelling." *Language Arts* 69 (October 1992): 418–424.

Strickland, Dorothy S. "Emergent Literacy: How Young Children Learn to Read." *Educational Leadership* (March 1990): 18–23.

Swisher, Karen. "An Action Model for Research in the Classroom: Developmental Spelling K–2." Paper presented at the annual meeting of the College Reading Association, Crystal City, VA, October 31, 1991 to November 3, 1991.

Templeton, Shane. "New Trends in an Historical Perspective: Old Story, New Resolution—Sound and Meaning in Spelling." *Language Arts* 69 (October 1992): 454–466.

---. "' Teaching and Learning the English Spelling System: Reconceptualizing Method and Purpose." *The Elementary School Journal* 92, No. 2 (1991): 185–201.

Texas Education Agency. *Spelling Instruction: A Proper Perspective.* n.p.: Texas Education Agency, Spring, 1991.

Tompkins, Gail E., and David B. Yaden, Jr. *Answering Students' Questions About Words.* Urbana, Illinois. ERIC Clearinghouse on Reading and Communication Skills and National Council of Teachers of English, 1986.

Wilde, Sandra. "An Analysis of the Development of Spelling and Punctuation in Selected Third and Fourth Grade Children": 1–47. Department of Language, Reading, and Culture, College of Education, University of Arizona, n.d.

---. "A Proposal for a New Spelling Curriculum." *The Elementary School Journal* 90, No. 3 (1990): 275–289.

---. "'Spelling Textbooks: A Critical Review." *Linguistics and Education* 2 (1990): 259-280.

---. *You Kan Red This!* Portsmouth: Heinemann, 1992.

Zutell, Jerry, and Timothy Rasinski. "Children's Spelling Strategies and Their Cognitive Development." *In Developmental and Cognitive Aspects of Learning to Spell: A Reflection of Word Knowledge.* Edited by Edmund H. Henderson and James W. Beers, 52–73. n.p.: International Reading Association, 1980.

---. "Reading and Spelling Connections in Third and Fifth Grade Students." *Reading Psychology: An International Quarterly* 10 (1989): 137–155.

Word Play and Language-Related List for Students

Agee, Jon. *Go Hang a Salami! I'm a Lasagna Hog! And Other Palindromes.* New York: Farrar, Straus, & Giroux, 1992.

Albert, Burton. *Code Busters!* Niles, IL: Albert Whitman, 1985.

Barrett, Judi. *A Snake Is Totally Tail.* New York: Atheneum, 1983.

Carroll, Lewis. *Jabberwocky.* Honsdale, PA: Caroline House, 1992.

Ciardi, John. *The Hopeful Trout & Other Limericks.* Boston: Houghton Mifflin, 1989, 1992.

Cole, William. *Poem Stew.* New York: HarperCollins, 1981, 1983.

Gackenbach, Dick. *Timid Timothy's Tongue Twister.* New York: Holiday House, 1986.

Hepworth, Cathi. *Antics! An Alphabetical Anthology.* New York: Putnam, 1992.

Hunt, Bernice K. *The Whatchmacallit Book.* New York: Putnam, 1976.

Kaye, Catherine Berger. *Word Works: Why the Alphabet Is a Kid's Best Friend.* Boston: Little, Brown and Company, 1985.

Keller, Charles. *Daffynitions.* Treehouse, 1978.

Kellogg, Steven. *Aster Aardvark's Alphabet Adventures.* New York: Morrow, 1987, 1992.

Lee, Dennis. *Alligator Pie.* Macmillan Canada, 1974.

Maestro, Guilio. *What's a Frank Frank? Tasty Homograph Riddles.* New York: Clarion, 1984.

---. *What's Mite Might? Homophone Riddles to Boost Your Word Power!* New York: Clarion, 1986.

Musgrove, Margaret. *Ashanti to Zulu: African Traditions.* New York: Clarion, 1988.

Terban, Marvin. *The Dove Dove: Funny Homograph Riddles.* New York: Clarion, 1988.

---. *Too Hot to Hoot: Funny Palindrome Riddles.* New York: Clarion, 1985.

Index

Index *(continued)*

Index *(continued)*